剑桥双语分级阅读·小说馆（第2版）

原版系列编辑 Philip Prowse

High Life, Low Life

贫富之间

[英] 艾伦·巴特斯比 著

李琳琳 编译

北京语言大学出版社
BEIJING LANGUAGE AND CULTURE UNIVERSITY PRESS

CAMBRIDGE UNIVERSITY PRESS

社图号25015

图书在版编目（CIP）数据

贫富之间 ： 英汉对照 / （英） 艾伦·巴特斯比 (Alan Battersby) 著 ； 李琳琳编译. -- 2版. -- 北京 ： 北京语言大学出版社, 2025. 3. -- (剑桥双语分级阅读小说馆). -- ISBN 978-7-5619-6734-8

Ⅰ. H319.4

中国国家版本馆CIP数据核字第2025LK8491号

贫富之间
PIN FU ZHI JIAN

责任编辑：赵敏亚
责任印制：周　燚

出版发行：北京语言大学出版社
社　　址：北京市海淀区学院路 15 号，100083
网　　址：www.blcup.com
电子信箱：service@blcup.com
电　　话：编 辑 部 010-8230 1019
发 行 部 010-8230 3650/3591/3648
北语书店 010-8230 3653
网购咨询 010-8230 3908
印　　刷：东港股份有限公司

版　　次：2017 年 6 月第 1 版　2025 年 3 月第 2 版　**印　　次**：2025 年 3 月第 1 次印刷
开　　本：880 毫米 × 1230 毫米　1/32　**印　　张**：6.5
字　　数：159 千字　**定　　价**：23.00 元

PRINTED IN CHINA
凡有印装质量问题，本社负责调换。售后QQ号1367565611，电话010-82303590

Preface

前言

“剑桥双语分级阅读·小说馆”是一套从剑桥大学出版社引进的面向非英语国家英语学习者的分级系列读物，由英语语言教学专家及小说作家合力创作。创作过程历时三十余年，出版后受到世界各地英语教师和英语学习者的喜爱，许多读本再版多次，三十余年来畅销不衰，成为受全球英语学习者青睐的优秀读本。

本系列读物具有以下突出特色：

1. 是原创英语读物，而非改编自普通作品的读物。因此，阅读本系列读物，我们读到的是原汁原味的原创英语，而非人为改编过的二手英语。

2. 是当代优秀短篇小说，而非年代久远的小说。因此，阅读本系列读物，我们读到的是当今鲜活的、学了就能用的英语，而非穿越时空的、学了用不上的英语；了解的是与读者同时代不同国家人们的生活和思想，而非隔代人的生活、文化和风土人情。

3. 是专为非英语国家的英语学习者量身定制的读物，而非为英语母语者所写的大众读物。因此，本系列读物是中国读者首选的英语学习读物。

4. 是英美知名小说家和英语语言教学专家合力创作的读物。小说家保障了读物的可读性与可欣赏性，英语语言教学专家保障了读物语言作为英语习得材料的科学性与可学性。本系列读物中的多个读本都曾在世界上颇具影响力的“语言学习者文学奖”(Language Learner Literature Award) 评选中获得大奖。因此，阅读本系列读物，我们会在欣赏小说的同时，自然而然地、有效地提高自己的英语水平。

5. 本系列读物的故事题材丰富多样，包括侦探、情感、历险、悬疑、人文、科幻、喜剧等，读者可以随心选择自己喜欢的类别阅读；故事内容生动有趣，故事情节引人入胜、扣人心弦，读者一旦开始阅读，就想一口气读完，使阅读真正升华到“悦读”。

6. 随书附赠的音频材料内容精彩，是专业配音员的演绎再创作。听着它，我们犹如在听广播剧、听评书，又仿佛是在听电影、听话剧……这种聆听英语的享受将彻底扫除学生对英语听力的畏难心理。

7. 本系列读物所使用的语言，既有英式英语，也有美式英语，对应的音频材料也相应分为英音和美音，读者可根据自己的喜好来选择。

8. 本系列近百本读物根据《欧洲语言共同参考框架》(CEFR) 和剑桥大学外语考评部开发的 ESOL 考试的标准来确定级别划分，是建立在科学研究和实践基础之上的分级。全套共分七个级别（与中国学生英语基础水平的大致对应关系，请参见图书封底表格），读者可根据自己的英语基础选择相应级别的读本来学习。

为了更好地帮助中国学生学习和欣赏，“剑桥双语分级阅读·小说馆”从剑桥大学出版社原版引进后又增加了以下内容：

1. 增加了适量的辅助学习内容，包括“读前思考”“读后活动”“学习指导”三个板块，其中“学习指导”板块又包括生词、短语和表达、文化点滴、阅读练习四项内容。增加这些板块的目的是全方位帮助学生提升英语阅读能力，扩充词汇量，扫除阅读中的文化障碍，增强对英语小说的鉴赏能力。

2. 增加了小说全文的参考译文。出于语言学习的考虑，译文多采用直译，但也尽量符合中文的表达习惯。

值得一提的是，所增加的辅助学习内容和参考译文，全部由来自全国不同省市知名中学（包括人大附中、北大附中、清华附中、黄冈中学、上海中学等三十余所中学）的一线英语教师完成。这些一线教师的加盟，确保了所加内容与中国学生的英语学习特点和学习需求相吻合，为学生阅读和欣赏读物、提高英语水平给予恰到好处的助力。

英语阅读是英语课堂的延伸和补充，也是培养英语语感、提高英语水平的有效途径。选择一套好的英语读物，收获的将不仅仅是语言的进步。欢迎年轻朋友们来到“剑桥双语分级阅读·小说馆”，打开一本本好书，品味一个个好故事，为实现梦想搭建桥梁。

北京语言大学出版社

Contents 目录

People in the story

故事中的人物

Nat Marley: New York private investigator

纳特·马利：纽约私家侦探

Stella Delgado: Nat Marley's personal assistant

斯特拉·德尔加多：纳特·马利的私人助理

Annie Clayton: a homeless woman

安妮·克莱顿：一个无家可归的女人

Mrs. Joanna Whittaker: a rich widow

乔安娜·惠特克夫人：一个有钱的寡妇

Martha Bianchi: Mrs. Whittaker's maid

玛莎·比安奇：惠特克夫人的女佣

Charlie Whittaker: Mrs. Whittaker's son

查利·惠特克：惠特克夫人的儿子

Betty Osborne: Mrs. Whittaker's daughter

贝蒂·奥斯本：惠特克夫人的女儿

Wilma Patterson: a lawyer

威尔玛·帕特森：一名律师

Jackie Robinson Clayton: Annie Clayton's son

杰基·罗宾森·克莱顿：安妮·克莱顿的儿子

Ernie Wiseman (Ernst Weissmann): a criminal

厄尼·怀斯曼（厄恩斯特·韦斯曼）：一名罪犯

Captain Oldenberg: detective with the New York Police Department (NYPD)

奥尔登伯格警监：纽约市警察局侦探

Joe Blaney: colleague of Nat Marley, ex-NYPD

乔·布兰尼：纳特·马利的同事，纽约市警察局前警员

Dr. Fischer: a doctor at Bellevue Hospital

费希尔医生：贝尔维尤医院的一名医生

Before reading

读前思考

1. Look at the title and picture on the front cover. What do you think *High Life, Low Life* means?

2. Are there parts of your town or city you have never visited? Why? Where are they?

3. Match the chapter titles and sentences from each chapter.

   ______ Chapter 1 Summer in the city

   ______ Chapter 2 Central Park West

   ______ Chapter 3 The will

   ______ Chapter 4 Beneath the city streets

   ______ Chapter 5 Inside information

   a) I'd heard of people living underground in New York, but I'd never seen it for myself.

   b) It was going to be another one of those hot, uncomfortable days.

   c) That's one expensive address.

   d) "I'd like to ask you a few questions about Mrs. Whittaker."

   e) "Nat, we have a problem," she said. "Mrs. Whittaker wants to make you rich."

4. If you have the recording, listen to Chapter 1.

Chapter 1
Summer in the city

They say if you don't like the heat, get out of the kitchen. New York, mid-July, if you don't like the heat, get out of the city. Anyone who could take a vacation was in the mountains or on Long Island. Anywhere cooler than the city. But me, I had work to do and dollars to earn. As I left my apartment building in Queens, the heat hit me. The temperature was already up in the eighties. Only seven o'clock in the morning and I was sweating. It was going to be another one of those hot, uncomfortable days. Time to catch the number seven train to Manhattan.

The name's Marley, Nat Marley. I know the city of New York like the back of my hand. New York is part of me; it's in my blood. During my fifteen years' service with the New York Police Department, I saw the best and worst of life in the city. After leaving the NYPD, I became a private investigator. Although I don't make that much money, I'm my own boss and I don't have to take orders from anybody. I prefer it that way.

At Grand Central Station, crowds of office workers hurried out to 42nd Street. There were usually a few homeless people in the station trying to make a few dollars before the police moved them along. When you make the same trip every day, you get to know people's faces. But today, I couldn't see any homeless people. Maybe they were out in the sunshine on 42nd Street.

Suddenly a voice called out, "Hey, Nat, don't you recognize me?"

I turned around. There was an old woman in an expensive-looking coat and skirt. It was Annie, a real New York character: one of the homeless people I'd known since I was a patrolman with the NYPD.

"Do you like my coat, Nat? I found it in the trash."

"A winter coat in July? You must be boiling. I like the coat, but you don't look too great, Annie."

"I'm OK, Nat. Anyway, a winter coat's valuable so it stays with me, sunshine or snow."

I looked at her closely. There was something different about her. I couldn't say what exactly. But she had changed.

"Sure you're feeling all right, Annie?"

"Me, Nat? Never felt better."

Maybe she was just exhausted from trying to earn a living on the streets at her age. But something told me I should stay around.

"I'll buy you breakfast. Coffee and doughnuts?" I offered.

Annie took my arm as we made our way toward the main entrance. Suddenly she pulled at my jacket.

"Hey, not so fast, Nat. Just give me a minute. It's this pain in my chest."

I looked at her closely. The sweat was pouring off her face. We hadn't walked far, but she was out of breath. She held my hand tightly. Her skin felt cold.

"Oh my God!" she cried.

She reached for her chest, her eyes and mouth wide open in pain. Then she fell at my feet, unconscious. A heart attack. I felt her wrist. There was no pulse. There was no movement from her chest either. She wasn't breathing. I didn't have time to think. All that NYPD training came back to me. First the breathing. Head back, hold the nose, open mouth, check the airway. Close my lips over the mouth. Breathe out, pause, and again. Then both hands on her chest. Push down. Again, fifteen times. I looked up at the circle of people around us.

"Someone call 911. Get an ambulance! Anyone here done first aid training?" I asked.

A guy stepped forward nervously. "I've just taken a first aid course," he said.

"Start with the breathing, then we'll change over."

We worked on her for five long minutes. I felt Annie's wrist again. This time there was a pulse. And then some movement in her chest. At last, I heard the sound of the ambulance siren.

The ambulance men took over and put Annie in the ambulance waiting on 42nd Street. I knew someone like her wouldn't have health insurance.

"You taking her to Bellevue Hospital?" I asked.

"Yeah."

"Here's my card. Any questions about hospital bills, tell them to call me."

How I would actually pay any hospital bills was another matter.

A police officer came over to interview me. As soon as he left me, a reporter from the *Daily News* ran up to me.

"Can I ask a few questions, sir? This is going to be a great story."

I didn't mind. The story might be good for business.

From Grand Central, it was five minutes' walk to my office at 220 East 43rd Street. Most offices in the building had their own air conditioning. Mine didn't, so it was hot and uncomfortable.

It was very quiet in the office when I arrived. No surprises there. Business is usually quiet in July. Even bad guys take vacations.

Stella Delgado, my personal assistant, was already at her desk. She looked tired and annoyed.

"Nat, when are we going to get air conditioning?" she asked. "It's impossible to work. And look at the sweat on your shirt!"

"I've been on my knees at Grand Central," I said, "saving an old lady's life. That's hard work in this heat."

I told Stella what had just happened. She stopped complaining about the heat.

"Let's go and see how she is," she suggested.

New York private investigators don't normally use public transportation. But I'm different. Stella and I took a number 15 bus downtown on Second Avenue then walked one block east to the hospital on First Avenue. I introduced myself to the receptionist.

"The name's Nat Marley. I'm a close friend of Annie

Clayton's. She's just been admitted to the emergency room. We have to see her, miss. You see ..."

"Sorry. Family only in the emergency room," the receptionist said.

"Look, miss. She's more like family to me than my own wife," I said.

That was true. I hadn't seen much of Mrs. Marley since the divorce.

"I'll call the emergency room and see what they say," replied the receptionist.

We were allowed to visit. Stella and I waited outside an examination room where a doctor was checking Annie's heart. Eventually the doctor came out and introduced herself.

"Mr. Marley? I'm Dr. Fischer. The rules say family only in here, but this is a special case. So you're the guy who saved Mrs. Clayton at Grand Central? You did a good job there."

"Is she going to be all right, Doctor?" I asked.

Her face told me all I needed to know. "She's a fighter, but she's had a serious heart attack," she said.

Annie was sleeping, and we waited over an hour before we were allowed in to see her. She looked exhausted but she smiled when she saw me.

"Nat, it's good to see you," she said. "And thanks."

"It was nothing, Annie. I save lives every day," I said.

"Nat, I've been thinking. I may not have much time left. This morning was no surprise. I've had heart trouble for years. Nat, can you find me a lawyer? I want to make a will."

I wondered what Annie had to leave anybody after she died. Anyway, I agreed to do as she asked. I knew an excellent family lawyer, Wilma Patterson. I called her and she agreed to come over to the hospital that afternoon.

This was the beginning of the strange story of two old ladies from the opposite ends of New York society – the high life and the low life. Two old ladies who had never met and whose lives were very different. This is the story of how those lives came together.

Chapter 2
Central Park West

The next morning, my picture was on an inside page of the *Daily News*, with the full story. It read "Dying Woman Saved." The story began:

"Yesterday, without the quick thinking of private investigator Nat Marley, Annie Clayton, a homeless New Yorker, would have died at Grand Central Station."

Around eleven o'clock, a messenger arrived with a letter. The address was written in very careful handwriting. I had a new job title:

"To Mr. Nat Marley, Senior Investigator, the Marley Investigation Agency."

"Wow, that makes you look important, Nat!" said Stella.

The letter was from Mrs. Joanna Whittaker, Apartment 1543, Century Apartments, 25 Central Park West. That's one expensive address. The Century Apartments were the last of the fashionable apartment buildings completed before the Great Depression of the 1930s.

The letter read:

Dear Mr. Marley,

I have just read about you in the Daily News. *I would like your agency to do a special service for me. I need a professional.*

I do not leave my apartment, and I wish to speak to you in private. The doorman will be expecting you. You may call on me any afternoon between 12:00 and 1:00.

Yours truly,
Joanna Whittaker (Mrs.)

"What do you think, Stella?" I asked.

"Interesting," said Stella.

"Shall we visit the lady? We could go now – nothing's happening here."

For once, I looked smart. I had put on a clean shirt and my good jacket, which was just back from the cleaner's. Stella was wearing her new suit. We looked like complete professionals.

"Stella, we're taking a cab," I said.

"A cab! Sure you're feeling all right?" she asked in surprise.

I'd never felt better. We could be visiting several million dollars so we had to look cool and fresh. Usually, I hate spending money on cabs, but if you want to look good in July, you don't walk.

It was 11:30 and the traffic wasn't moving much quicker than you could walk. I felt sorry for the cab drivers. We drove slowly across town and up to Columbus Circle, then uptown along Central Park West to Century Apartments. One of the best addresses in Manhattan.

When we got there I gave my name to the doorman.

"Mrs. Whittaker's expecting you, Mr. Marley. But I'll have to warn her first. Don't want the old lady to get too excited."

He picked up the phone. Nothing for over a minute.

"This could take some time," the doorman explained.

"She sometimes gets confused. Hello. Is this Martha? It's Bob in the lobby. I have some visitors for Mrs. Whittaker ... Yes, Mr. Nathan Marley and his personal assistant Ms. Stella Delgado ... Yes, I'll send them up."

Inside the elevator, it was all dark wood, thick carpets and mirrors. If this was just the elevator, imagine what the apartments were like. Would I ever live in a place like this? On my income, only in my dreams. I rang the bell of the apartment and waited. A minute later, I rang again. Eventually the door opened. A large middle-aged woman stared at me unpleasantly.

"You Mr. Marley?" she asked.

"Yes, ma'am. With my assistant Ms. Stella Delgado."

"Show me your license."

I passed her my private investigator's license.

"Just a minute," she said and shut the door in my face.

Another wait. She returned, and without a word showed us in to the living room where an old lady was waiting.

"Mr. Marley and Miss Delgado, how do you do? I'm Joanna Whittaker. Do sit down. Martha, tea for our guests."

I looked around the room which was full of beautiful 1940s furniture. Nothing had been changed for years and I felt like I was in an old Hollywood movie. I wondered who would walk in next – Cary Grant or Joan Crawford?

Martha returned with cups and two teapots. She didn't exactly look pleased to receive visitors. Her thick, strong arms held the heavy tea things with no effort at all.

"Assam or Darjeeling tea, Mr. Marley?" asked Mrs.

Whittaker.

I wasn't sure of the difference, but I wasn't about to admit that.

"Assam, thank you, ma'am. Three sugars."

"Oh good! I like a man with a sweet tooth. Just like my poor husband used to have. And you, Miss Delgado?"

"Darjeeling, please," Stella replied.

"My husband took this place when we were married," said Mrs. Whittaker. "I've lived here ever since. At one time, this apartment was full of laughter and happiness. But since my poor husband died there's just been myself and Martha. Martha does everything for me – I never leave the apartment. She's been with the family for years. She's almost part of the furniture."

There was a sound of glass breaking in the kitchen. Mrs. Whittaker didn't hear it. Someone didn't like being called part of the furniture.

"Do you have any family?" asked Stella.

"A son and a daughter. They don't live in the city. Charlie's in Albany and Betty's in Syracuse. I'd like to see more of them. Especially the grandchildren, but ..."

The old lady's eyes filled with tears. Stella took her hand. She knew exactly what to do. I'm no good in situations like these.

"Now don't cry, ma'am. We understand," said Stella.

"Do you? ... I'm sorry, Miss."

"No need to apologize," I said.

"Thank you. I'm all right," she said. Then she looked at me. "Now, Tom," she said, "let's get down to business."

"Tom?" I asked, looking back at her.

"Did I say Tom?" she asked. "Oh, silly me! My mistake. You know, you look so much like my poor dead husband. Now where was I? Oh, yes, Mr. Marley, I need a lawyer."

Chapter 3
The will

"Mrs. Whittaker," I said, "I'm not a lawyer."

"I may be old, but I'm not completely stupid," the old lady replied. "I want you to *find* me a lawyer."

"Where's the phone book?" I asked. "I'll show you who to call."

"You don't understand. I want you to find a good lawyer and bring him here. Someone I can trust. It's to do with my will."

Mrs. Whittaker opened her handbag and took out a pile of hundred-dollar bills. I hadn't seen so much money in one place in years.

"What's your fee, Mr. Marley?"

"It's one thousand dollars a day plus expenses. But not just now, ma'am. When I finish the job. I wouldn't carry all that money around. It could be dangerous."

We left the coolness of the lobby at the Century Apartments and walked out onto Central Park West. If you don't like the heat, find a bar. Which is what we did. A short walk through the park to the Tavern on the Green. Not the sort of place I would choose to drink in. Expensive drinks and too many tourists. But it was close. That's important when it's hot enough to fry an egg on the sidewalk.

We sat in a quiet corner with a couple of cold beers and talked about the two women we had just met.

"What a way to live!" said Stella.

"Yeah. Can you imagine it? Never going outside," I replied. "As far as I can see, Martha does everything for Mrs. Whittaker. She looks as if she's got the strength. Strange woman, though. I wouldn't want to meet Martha on a dark lonely street."

Stella remained silent. I could see she was thinking.

"There's something very strange about Mrs. Whittaker, too," she said finally. "She's got family, so why doesn't she have her own family lawyer? And I couldn't see any photos of her children. Just wedding photos and pictures of her husband. Then she called you "Tom." Who does she think you are? Her husband returned from the dead?"

"Who knows what's going on!" I said. "But worrying about it isn't going to earn us any money. Let's go and find that lawyer."

Stella and I went back to the office and I made a call to Wilma Patterson. By three o'clock we had made the arrangements. We met Wilma back at the Century Apartments and took the elevator up to the fifteenth floor. Martha showed us in without a word.

"Ah, Mr. Marley and Miss Delgado. But where is my lawyer?" asked Mrs. Whittaker.

Wilma stopped her. "Mrs. Whittaker, I am Wilma Patterson, senior partner of Patterson and Schofield, attorneys-at-law."

"I don't believe you!" Mrs. Whittaker said sharply.

"Mrs. Whittaker," I said, "Mrs. Patterson is the finest lawyer I know. Trust me."

Mrs. Whittaker looked at me doubtfully. I just nodded and smiled. Eventually she relaxed.

"Well, well. These modern times. I wasn't expecting a lady lawyer. Now do sit down. You will join me in a glass of sherry, won't you? Martha!"

Martha came in with bottles and glasses. She looked angry. Mrs. Whittaker waved her away to the kitchen without so much as a "thank you."

"Sweet or dry, Mr. Marley?" she asked.

I don't drink sherry, but I didn't want to upset Mrs. Whittaker. I asked for sweet.

"A very good choice, Tom," she said, smiling. "Oh dear! There I go again, calling you Tom. Now Tom always enjoyed a sweet sherry. And you do too. Now Mr. Marley, if you would wait here with Miss Delgado. I have business to discuss with Mrs. Patterson in the library."

I knew this was going to take time. I made myself comfortable and had a couple more sherries. After a while, Stella fell asleep. I started putting prices on the furniture in the living room and lost count at $50,000.

An hour later, Wilma returned, looking worried. "Nat, we have a problem," she said. "Mrs. Whittaker wants to make you rich."

"Is that a problem?" I asked.

"It is when the son and daughter don't get a cent. I've talked it over with her, but she won't listen. She wants it all to go to you. She read about you in the papers. Says you remind her of her late husband, Tom. Says she couldn't think of a better person to leave everything to."

The door to the kitchen was open. Suddenly there was the sound of more glass breaking. Did Martha have a lot of accidents, or was she listening to every word that was being said and didn't like what she heard?

"So what happens now?" I asked.

"In the end, I don't have much choice," said Wilma.

"A lawyer has to follow the client's instructions."

"I don't like this," I said. "You've got to speak to the family and arrange a meeting. Or else I'm going to be in the middle of a family war."

"Agreed," she replied. "But I'm not making any promises."

Wilma went back in the library. Then I heard the sound of someone using an old typewriter. A couple more sherries later, I was starting to get a headache. I got up and looked more closely at one of the photos of Tom Whittaker. Forty-something, a little fat, and losing his hair. Just like me, unfortunately. The sound of typing went on. At five o'clock, Wilma came out to ask Stella to sign the will as a witness and the doorman was called from downstairs to be the second witness. A few minutes later, everybody was back in the sitting room. Mrs. Whittaker looked pleased.

"Thank you, everybody," Mrs. Whittaker said. "Mr. Marley, your fee."

She gave me a fat envelope.

"Mrs. Patterson has already given me her bill." Mrs. Whittaker gave Wilma another fat envelope.

"Now, before you leave, a present for everybody. Martha ... *Martha*!"

Martha entered with a pile of large books in her powerful arms.

"In memory of my dear husband," said Mrs. Whittaker.

I looked at the title: *A History of Whittaker Air* by Tom Whittaker, President. So that was where the family money came from.

"Thank you so much, ma'am. I'll enjoy reading this," I lied.

Mrs. Whittaker gave me a big sweet smile. Almost like she was in love. It frightened me. She took my hand. Her hand was all bone and paper-thin skin. At that point, I just wanted to get out of that apartment and never return.

"You'll enjoy living here when I'm gone, Tom," she said.

Martha was standing behind everybody. She gave Mrs. Whittaker a long dark look.

Finally we escaped into the late afternoon heat. Outside, I opened the envelope, two thousand dollars in hundred-dollar bills. Not bad for one day's work.

Wilma Patterson looked worried.

"Nat, once the family finds out about the will, there's going to be trouble," she said.

"Don't I know it!" I replied. "You've got to get the family talking. Get her to change the will."

"As I said before, I'll try," Wilma replied.

"Thanks," I said. "I don't want anyone to think I take advantage of confused old ladies."

Chapter 4
Beneath the city streets

By the time we got back to East 43rd Street, it was past six o'clock. No point trying to do any work. I wandered over to McFadden's Bar on Second Avenue. The usual crowd of *Daily News* reporters was there, doing what they did best – drinking.

I needed information and I knew just the guy who could help – Ed Winchester. He used to be the crime reporter at the *Daily News*, and he still did some part-time work. Once a reporter, always a reporter.

"Nat, my old friend!" Ed said when he saw me. "You've arrived at just the right moment."

"Does that mean your glass is empty, Ed?" I asked, and waved to the bartender. "Jack! Sam Adams for me and a drink for Ed."

It was time for Ed to earn his drink. I told him about our strange meeting with Mrs. Whittaker and the business of the will. I asked what he knew about the family. I knew I could depend on Ed – he had a very long memory.

Ed took a drink and said, "Hmm ... Tom Whittaker. Now, he's the guy who started one of the first regular air services between New York and Chicago in the 1920s. The business became very successful in the 1950s and 1960s. Then he sold it. I think it became part of Pan Am. I'll see what else I can find out."

"So the family's got money?" I asked.

"Lots of it," Ed said.

It had been a long day and I was getting a headache. I left and took the number seven train home to Queens. I couldn't eat much of the takeout meal I got from the diner down the block. That night, I lay awake for hours. It was dawn before I finally fell asleep. In the morning, I didn't feel very active. I went off to work like a machine. Not a thought or an idea in my head. Take my advice – avoid New York in July.

When I arrived at the office, Stella was already at work. Inside, it didn't feel as hot as usual. There were two electric fans on her desk. I could see through the door to my office. Another two fans.

"Morning, Stella. Where did those fans come from?" I asked.

"Macy's," she replied. "I phoned yesterday. They

were the last ones in the store. We were lucky to get them. Here's the bill."

"What's this?" I asked. "Two hundred dollars! Do you think I'm made of money?"

"I can't work if I don't have the fans," said Stella. "If I can't work, I don't make you any money. It's as simple as that."

I was about to argue when the phone rang. It was Dr. Fischer at Bellevue Hospital. Annie was asking to see me. Apparently, it was important.

When I got to Annie's room, she was sitting up in bed, but she looked awful. There was a visitor with her.

"Nat, it's good to see you," Annie said weakly. "This is Leona, an old friend. Leona, meet Nat. He's going to help me with some family business. And before you ask, Nat, I'll pay you somehow."

"I wouldn't dream of asking for money, Annie," I said. I was there to help out an old friend. Annie was already sick enough without knowing what my daily fee was.

"A man can't put food on the table by working for nothing," Annie said. "Nat, I want you to go with Leona. She's going to take you somewhere you've never been before."

In my fifteen years' service with the NYPD, I'd been to most places in New York City. I wondered where Leona was going to take me. We left the hospital and walked four blocks west to the subway station on 28th Street. Then we took an uptown number six train to 103rd Street and Lexington. Some New Yorkers never go further uptown than 96th Street on the East Side. For them, anywhere north is like a foreign country. At 103rd Street, it does feel like another world. There are no expensive stores, good restaurants, or skyscrapers. The only tall buildings are the housing projects, low cost apartments built for working people. The people on the streets are mostly African-American and Latino.

"So what's new, Leona?" I asked. "I used to walk these streets when I was a patrolman."

"Just be patient, Nat," she replied. "You ain't seen nothing yet."

Leona took me across Lexington to an old building. It looked empty. But the door opened as soon as Leona knocked. A big man welcomed Leona, but then looked at me with a cold stare, pointed, and asked, "What's this guy doing here?"

"He's OK," explained Leona. "He's cool. Nat's doing a little job for Annie."

Leona took me down some steps. At the bottom there was a hole in the wall and she led me through it. I could hardly see my hand in front of my face.

"Where are we, Leona?" I asked.

"Below the streets. This is the city you don't know. Careful now, there's a train coming."

A downtown number five train passed. The light from the train windows helped me see where we were – the subway. There were four train tracks, two uptown and two downtown and a narrow path beside the tracks. Ahead of us was a subway station, but no lights.

"Welcome to our home, Nat," Leona said. "This station isn't used anymore, so we moved in."

I'd heard of people living underground in New York, but I'd never seen it for myself. I could see a light ahead. "Home" was an old, wooden change booth, the type I remember from my childhood. A woman was sitting in an armchair by the door.

"Ellie, this guy's a friend. He's helping Annie with some family business. I'll put some coffee on."

"You know what?" I said, looking around. "You've got a nice place down here. Better than my place in Queens. You live down here all the time?" I asked.

"Sure we do," replied Ellie. "Cool in the summer and we manage to keep warm in the winter. And we don't pay rent."

"Are you safe down here?"

"We've lived on the streets," Leona said. "I can tell you, it's safer underground. Everyone knows each other here. If a stranger comes, we know about it. The subway workers know us. They leave us alone."

Leona started moving piles of black plastic bags. Underneath was an old metal box with a lock.

"Nat," she said, "Annie wants you to take this box to her."

Leona took me back up to the street. As I traveled back downtown to 28th Street, I wondered how many more underground communities I was passing on the subway.

Back at the hospital, I gave Annie the box. Then she took out a key that was tied around her neck, unlocked the box, and showed me a photograph of a cheerful teenage boy.

"Nat," said Annie, "this is my son, Jackie. I haven't seen him in twenty years. I want you to find him."

"I never knew you had family," I said.

"You don't know everything about me. I may not

have long to live, Nat, and I want to see him again before I die. We lived in a housing project in the South Bronx. Not a nice area. After leaving home, Jackie used to visit now and then. Usually to borrow money. I knew he wasn't a good kid, but he's my son. His father was the top man in an office where I once worked as a cleaner. The sort of guy who tells every woman his wife doesn't understand him. I was lonely and we had a good time. He made me laugh, and Jackie's the result."

"How old is he now?" I asked.

"Born in 1954, so about your age," Annie said. "I last saw him in Riker's Island jail in 1979. He'd been stealing cars and getting into fights. It's easy to find the wrong type of friends in the Bronx. When I visited him in jail, he said he never wanted to see me again. It broke my heart. From that point, my life went to pieces. I was feeling really low and that's when I started living on the streets of Manhattan. I had to escape, get out of the Bronx, and forget."

"Anything else you can tell me?" I asked.

"I once heard he was living on the Lower East Side," she said. "Working as a cab driver."

"A cab driver, you say? If he had a police record he

couldn't get a job as a cab driver. His full name?"

"Jackie Robinson Clayton."

"Height?" I asked.

"About five feet ten inches," Annie said weakly. "Oh, and he's got a tattoo of a bird, the American eagle, on his left arm. When you find him, tell him his mother wants to see him. Bring him here. It's important."

"I'll do my best, Annie," I said, "but don't raise your hopes too much. This could be a difficult one."

Annie gave me the photo and locked the box. Then she asked me to take the box and key to Wilma Patterson's office. She lay back on the bed, sweating and breathing heavily. I called the nurse. Annie looked more dead than alive.

Chapter 5
Inside information

I got to McFadden's Bar at lunchtime. Inside, it was noisy and busy, but cool, thanks to the air conditioning. I realized I was hungry. I hadn't eaten properly since breakfast the day before. I ordered a steak with extra fries. As I was eating, Jack, the bartender, called me.

"Hey, Nat, there's a guy here says you're buying him a drink." I looked up. Ed Winchester was waving an empty glass.

"Well, I guess I am," I said. "Over here, Ed. And this had better be good."

"I like doing business this way," said Ed. "You buy me drinks and I find you information."

Ed told me he'd been in the *Daily News* library, reading up about Whittaker Air. It was a good story. Tom Whittaker was an interesting guy. He had been a U.S. Air Service pilot and was shot down in France in the First World War. He was one of the lucky few who made it home. When he got out of the air service, he bought a couple of ex-air service planes and started flying people around the city. Sightseeing by air. In the late 1920s he started an airline business. Flights to Washington and Chicago. He saw that the future was air travel. During the 1950s the railroads were beginning to lose passengers to the airlines and Whittaker Air was taking a big share of them.

"Was he the sort of guy who lived for his work?" I asked.

"Not at all," replied Ed. "He was quite a ladies' man. Look at this: *Daily News,* 1957."

Ed gave me a photocopy of a newspaper story. There was Tom Whittaker at a table in a cocktail bar with three amazing-looking blondes. Each one better built and better looking than Marilyn Monroe. Whittaker looked pleased with himself. I could understand why.

"Just look at him," said Ed. "He could be your brother."

"We might look alike," I said, "but he had everything I don't have. Money and women."

Ed went on to tell me that Tom Whittaker worked hard and played hard. Even after he was married he played around with other women. It wasn't a happy marriage and he and Mrs. Whittaker probably stayed together for the children. He sold Whittaker Air to Pan

Am in the late 1960s. Then he spent most of his time on City Island, drinking and fishing. He died in 1974.

"Goodbye, Tom Whittaker," I said.

"You're in luck, buddy," said Ed. "When she dies, you can afford drinks for everyone."

I walked back to East 43rd Street. Stella was busy at the computer when I arrived at the office.

"Hi, Stella," I said. "I've just been speaking to Ed."

"Don't you mean speaking and drinking?" Stella replied.

"Yeah. With Ed you can't do one without the other."

I told Stella everything I'd learned from Ed.

"You know, Nat, it frightens me. Mrs. Whittaker, Martha, that apartment," she said.

"Uh-huh. Like something out of a horror movie."

"You said it," Stella added. "And imagine never going out. What sort of life is that? Mrs. Whittaker's not right in the head."

"She isn't if she's left money to me," I said. "Any clients for me to see?"

"The phone hasn't rung all day," said Stella.

"Oh well. I'm going to Century Apartments to see the one person I know there who's not crazy. Bob the doorman."

I arrived at Century Apartments and walked into the lobby. The air conditioning was working perfectly. It was like walking into December.

"Bob, remember me?" I asked.

"Ah, Mr. Marley," he said.

"Call me Nat. I'd like to ask you a few questions about Mrs. Whittaker."

"Now, Mr. Marley ... Nat," he said. "I really shouldn't talk about our ..."

"Would this help?" I asked.

I showed him my investigator's license. That helped a little. I also showed him a fifty-dollar bill. That helped a lot.

"Why, thank you," he said.

"How does Mrs. Whittaker get everything she needs?" I asked.

"Martha does some of the shopping, or the stores send things to the apartment. Mrs. Whittaker is the type of lady who likes to be looked after."

"Does she get many visitors?"

"I've been here five years," Bob said. "In that time, the only visitors I've seen are her son and daughter. Even they've only been here three or four times. The last time I saw them was over two years ago. I remember because they were both angry when they left. The daughter was in tears. Family disagreement or something."

So Mrs. Whittaker saw nobody except for Martha, I thought. Not a healthy way of life.

Chapter 6
East Village

Now and then the elevator breaks down at the office. This was one of those days. After walking up eight floors, I felt hot and uncomfortable. The fans didn't make much difference. Fall couldn't come soon enough.

I had phone calls to make. At last, real work – finding a missing person – Annie's son, Jackie. My first call was to Police Headquarters. I knew someone who could help, someone I used to work with. That is, if he wasn't feeling too bad tempered.

"Get me Captain Oldenberg, will you?"

"Marley!" Oldenberg shouted, "I've got enough problems without you calling me."

"You don't sound happy in your work," I said. "Listen, I'm trying to find a missing person, a Jackie Robinson Clayton. He's been in trouble. He was in Riker's Island in 1979. He may be working as a cab driver now. Forty-six years old, medium height, the American eagle on his left arm."

"Anything else?" Oldenberg asked.

"Nothing," I said. "His mother hasn't seen him in twenty years. And Oldenberg, this is a job for an old friend."

"OK, Marley," said Oldenberg. "But I'm not lifting a finger in this heat. I'll get Lieutenant Brandstein to do it."

"First thing," I said, "get him to check if the guy's in prison, will you?"

Next I needed some information from the *Daily News*. I put a call through to Ed Winchester. Luckily, he was back from McFadden's Bar.

"Nat, what can I do for you?" he asked.

"I'm trying to find a guy by the name of Jackie Robinson Clayton," I said. "He's been in trouble, so there might be some news stories on him."

I gave Ed the information he needed. I crossed my fingers and hoped he would turn up something.

The phone rang as soon as I put it down. Lieutenant Brandstein was doing a good job. Jackie Clayton was not in jail anywhere in the U.S.A. We were doing well. I was beginning to enjoy myself. This was what life as a private investigator should be like. I even forgot how hot it was. Now I needed some extra help. Joe Blaney was just the guy. He was a big tough ex-cop who did work for me sometimes.

"Joe, it's Nat. Listen, my life is full of old ladies at the moment. I've got a strange client – a Mrs. Joanna Whittaker. And Martha, who lives with her, is even stranger. I need to know more about them." I gave Joe the story so far with the address and descriptions.

"Boss," Joe said, "You sure do meet some crazy people."

I spent the next morning looking around the Lower East Side, trying to find Jackie. Often, when you turn over a stone, you find something unpleasant beneath it. It can be the same with families. The more you find out, the more dirt you discover. I was hoping this wasn't going to happen with Jackie.

No luck at any of the cab companies or bars I visited. How far could you get looking for a guy in his mid-forties using a photo of him as a teenager? Finally, I found a cab driver on Canal Street in Chinatown who'd heard of Jackie. He told me to try the East Village.

I started on Avenues A, B and C, once known as Alphabet City. It was a total waste of time until I got to Vazac's Bar on Avenue B.

I showed the bartender Jackie's picture. When I told him about the tattoo, I could see he'd heard of him. He gave me a dark look.

"You a cop or something?" he asked.

"No, buddy," I said. "The name's Marley. Just an honest private investigator."

I showed him my license.

"I don't talk to cops or private eyes, mister," the bartender said.

"Nice friendly place you got here. A guy could feel very welcome. Do you talk to money?"

I turned my license round. Behind it was a twenty-dollar bill. As the bartender reached for it, I pulled my hand away.

"Not so fast. What've you got?" I asked.

"OK, I know him," he said. "Haven't seen him recently. He's got money, but it doesn't come from driving a cab."

"Oh yeah?" I said. "So where does it all come from?"

"Buying what people steal," he replied. "If you got something hot, go to Jackie. Don't make him angry though – he's tough."

"Do you know who he works for?" I asked.

"Do I get my twenty bucks now?"

"Tell me who he works for," I said.

"Try Wiseman Cabs on Avenue A," said the bartender. "Just uptown from Tompkins Square Park."

I dropped the twenty-dollar bill onto the bar and walked out. I knew Tompkins Square Park well. When I was a patrolman, the park had been home to most of the homeless of the East Village. They used to call the community "Tent City." Later, they were moved on, but not without a fight, and the place was cleaned up. I found the cab office. There were a couple of cabs parked outside. I pretended to be a tourist. The guy at the desk gave me a poisonous look.

"Can you help me, mister?" I asked. "I'm on vacation. First visit to the Big Apple. I want to hire a cab for the day so I can do some real sightseeing."

The guy behind the desk looked as if he hadn't slept, washed, or shaved for days. He smelled even worse than me. He lit a cigarette then coughed for a full fifteen seconds. Finally, he was able to speak.

"Mister, we don't hire cabs out for the day," he said.

"Hey," I said. "Is this a cab company or what?"

"I repeat, we don't do it. You stupid or something?"

One thing was clear. Wiseman Cabs didn't want customers. Certainly not the sort of customers who wanted to hire cabs. They were in another line of business and I wanted to know what. I decided to surprise him.

"Mr. Wiseman?" I said.

"How do you know my name?"

"Could be something to do with the sign outside," I replied and then continued, "I'm looking for Jackie Clayton."

"Oh yeah?" he said. "What do you want with him?"

"It's private. Family business," I said.

"Well it just so happens I'm looking for him too, and when I find him I'll ..." He stopped as if he had said more than he had intended.

"You'll do what?" I asked.

"Get out of here!" Wiseman shouted. "I don't know why I'm talking to you. Don't stick your big nose in here again!"

I got the feeling I wasn't welcome anymore. I left and called Joe Blaney on my cell phone.

"Nat here. What sort of morning have you had, Joe?"

"Great. Just had coffee and cake with Mrs. Whittaker."

"How did you manage that, Joe?"

"Easy. I know a guy who runs a flower shop on East

28th. I bought some flowers and wrote a note saying 'From your special friend Nat Marley.' Then I borrowed his shop coat and pretended I was the guy from the flower shop. That way I got up to the apartment. As soon as I said the flowers were from Mr. Marley, the old lady never stopped talking. She thinks you're wonderful."

"I know," I said. "It's troubling, isn't it?"

"Then I got Mrs. Whittaker talking about her family. She thinks the world of her late husband. I tried to get her to talk about the children, but she just said that they won't visit anymore. I got her son's phone numbers from the address book on the hall table. Easy."

"That's good work, Joe. Now, I've got another job. I want you to watch Wiseman Cabs on Avenue A. Jackie used to work for them. There's something strange going on. They wouldn't let me hire a cab, so I want to know how they make their money. And get some photos."

Joe had given me work and home numbers for Charlie Whittaker. Maybe Wilma Patterson could get the Whittaker family talking. I called her office with the phone numbers. It was early evening before she got back to me.

"Nat? Wilma here. I managed to talk to Charlie Whittaker. He said they used to bring his children to visit until it got too painful. It was the way Mrs. Whittaker kept talking about her late husband, as if he were some kind of god. The truth of the matter is that it was a loveless marriage. Tom never had time for his children. In fact, Charlie says he was like a stranger to them."

"What a way to grow up," I said.

"Charlie Whittaker's agreed to try and set up a family meeting," Wilma continued. "His mother refuses to talk to him over the phone, so he'll have to visit. All this will take time. And will she agree? It's doubtful."

"Well, this is a fine mess!" I said.

"Don't blame yourself, Nat."

Chapter 7 Developments

It had been a long day. It was almost time for a cold beer. Stella was reading at her desk.

"How are things, Stella?" I asked.

"Everything's fine except that the office is too hot," Stella replied. "I can't work and I've got a headache."

"Message received. So everything's normal," I said. "That's what I like to hear. What are you reading about?"

"Air-conditioning units. You know what they are – smart machines that cool down rooms." She held a picture of one up.

"Dream on! These things cost money," I said.

The phone rang. It was Joe.

"Nat? I've been watching Wiseman Cabs all afternoon. There's a lot of movement in and out of that office. Cab drivers going in carrying one suitcase then coming out with a different one, and driving away. Seem to be doing everything except carrying passengers."

"Interesting. I wonder what Wiseman's up to?"

"The answer's in those suitcases, boss."

"Did you get some photos?" I asked.

"Used a whole roll of film. It's being developed now," Joe replied.

"Well done. There'll be a cold beer with your name on it waiting at McFadden's."

Why pay for a sauna when all you have to do is sit and sweat in your office? Maybe Stella was right. She was usually right about a lot of things. I was just thinking about the cold beers when Dr. Fischer phoned from Bellevue Hospital. Annie's condition was getting much worse.

"How much longer has she got, Doctor?" I asked.

"She's had heart trouble for years, and then with that heart attack at the station ... I'm seriously worried, Mr. Marley."

"Is she still conscious?"

"Yes, but only just."

"Well, I've got something that should make her hold on," I said. "We're looking for her son and getting closer. We've found his old boss in the East Village. There seems to have been some argument between them. My guess is Jackie's keeping away from him. Just tell her we're getting close."

I felt both sad and angry as I put down the phone. Sad for the people who had to live out their lives on the streets. Angry about the society that put them on the streets.

Stella stopped reading and looked up.

"What's the matter, Nat?"

"It's Annie. If we don't find Jackie soon, she's going to die without seeing him," I said.

"Nat, I got an idea."

"Yeah?"

"Why don't I phone every cab company in the book? I could say I'm Jackie's ex-girlfriend wanting to see him again, to talk things over," Stella said.

"Good thinking. But first, I need some food and beer. I'll see you in McFadden's after you've locked up."

Ed Winchester from the *Daily News* was watching me as I finished my first beer. It was cool and delicious and hardly touched the sides of my throat as it went down. I immediately felt better.

"Nat, what a thirst! Now, have I got something for you. From the *Daily News*, five years ago. But first ..."

"I get it. The story's going to cost me another drink. This had better be good."

Ed handed me a photocopy of a news story. The

headline read "Weissmann and Clayton Not Guilty." I continued reading. "Ernst Weissmann and Jackie Clayton walked free today after being found not guilty of buying and selling stolen property."

"That's it," I said. "Joe spent the afternoon watching what was going on at Wiseman Cabs. Jackie Clayton used to work for Wiseman Cabs. In this story,

Jackie was with a guy called Weissmann. Maybe he changed his name to make it sound more American."

Joe had arrived with the photos. Picture after picture of cab drivers going in and out of the office with different suitcases. And a beautiful picture of Wiseman.

"That's him," I said. "Now if we compare him with the picture of Ernst Weissmann in the *Daily News* story. Yeah, it's the same guy. And he doesn't get any prettier with age. This is NYPD work. Excuse me while I phone Captain Oldenberg."

Oldenberg was in a bad mood. He sounded as if he

was about to explode. That was normal and natural. I only got worried when he was in a good mood.

"What do you want, Marley? Don't waste my time."

"Oldenberg, you remember a guy by the name of Weissmann? He was found not guilty about five years ago."

"Yeah. I'd love to get my hands on him again."

"Your dreams may come true. Get some of your boys to watch Wiseman Cabs on Avenue A. I think Weissmann, or Wiseman as he's known now, is still in the same kind of work, with the cab business as a cover."

"This sounds promising, Marley."

"And if you get Weissmann, give him a hard time."

"Trust me, Marley. What have you got against him?" Oldenberg asked.

"He refused to let me hire a cab."

I knew from my time with the NYPD that Oldenberg was one of the most unpleasant people I'd ever meet. The strange thing was that I liked the guy. As long as you stayed on the right side of him, things were all right.

There was a beer waiting for me at the bar. I always have close relationships with beers.

"How's Oldenberg?" asked Joe.

"He's in a terrible mood," I answered.

"So what's new?"

Stella arrived and had brought another magazine about air conditioning. She showed me the front cover. It read: "You too can be cool, fresh, and relaxed in July. Say goodbye to the summer time blues with Antarctic Air Conditioning. Two units for under seven hundred dollars."

Under seven hundred dollars? The price was six hundred and ninety-nine. That made my temperature rise. But I knew I had lost. If it would keep Stella happy, it was well worth it.

"That's it! You win, Stella. Do it before I change my mind," I said.

"What's going on, boss?" asked Joe.

"Nat has kindly agreed to get air conditioning for the office," said Stella.

I was going to be seven hundred dollars poorer. That made me feel very sad indeed. Like when you lose a close friend. It looked like I was going to spend Mrs. Whittaker's two thousand dollars before it even reached my bank account.

Chapter 8

A death in the family

That night I tried to get some sleep. I remembered an idea I'd heard. Take an electric fan. Fill a bowl with plenty of ice. Put the fan behind the bowl. Turn on the fan and wait for cool air. That's what's supposed to happen. It was a small improvement until the ice turned to water. That didn't take long and I didn't have any more ice. Another sleepless night. I gave up at 3:00 AM. I could stay home and feel exhausted or go into the office and feel exhausted. At least it would be cooler traveling to work in the middle of the night.

The New York subway never stops working. And since the Mayor cleaned up the city, it's a lot safer. I didn't worry about using it at this time. At 4:00 AM, midtown Manhattan feels like another city. There's almost no-one on the streets. Even the air smells fresh. At the office, I opened the windows and turned on all the fans. Finally, I got some sleep. Stella found me there, still asleep at 8:00 AM.

"Nat!" she shouted. "Have you been drinking?"

"Honest, Stella," I said sleepily, "I couldn't sleep at home. I suppose you slept well?"

"I always do. Go out and get yourself some breakfast, Nat. And bring me back a coffee, will you?"

Outside, I could already feel the heat rising from the sidewalks. I was back in twenty minutes with coffee and doughnuts. The walk didn't do me much good. Now Stella had all four electric fans going in her office.

"Hey! Don't I even get a fan now?" I asked.

"Take them, Nat," Stella said. "I just borrow your two fans when you're out. There's a message from Dr. Fischer about Annie. No change from last night."

"She's a fighter," I said. "She's holding on for Jackie."

The phone rang. I didn't recognize the voice.

"Mr. Marley? This is Miss Bianchi at Century Apartments. You know me as Martha. The woman who takes the orders. Well, there ain't going to be no orders to take now. The old lady's dead."

"Oh?" I said. "You all right, Martha?"

"Of course I'm all right," she said. "But she ain't. She's cold."

"I'll be right there," I told her.

Things were moving too quickly for my liking. I turned to Stella. "Mrs. Whittaker has died. Close the office and let's get over there."

At Century Apartments, Bob the doorman was as surprised as I had been. It was the first he had heard about Mrs. Whittaker's death. He phoned up to the apartment. Two minutes later we were at the door. This time we got in quickly. Then, another surprise. Martha was smiling.

"Tell me what happened?" I asked.

"Sure," Martha said. "I went in with Mrs. Whittaker's morning tea, and there she was. Cold and dead. Come and take a look."

"I'll stay here," said Stella, with her hand to her mouth.

Mrs. Whittaker was in her bed. Her mouth and eyes were wide open and her skin was gray. She was very dead.

"Feel her," said Martha, lifting Mrs. Whittaker's thin arm. "She's cold."

"I'll take your word for it, Martha. And don't touch the body again. Has the doctor already seen her?"

"Why should he? Not much he can do for her now."

"What? Call the doctor now!"

While Martha was out of the room making the call, I had a quick look around. There was a bottle of pills on the bedside table. To help her sleep? I'd check on that. Everything else seemed to be completely normal. I had Charlie Whittaker's number and asked Stella to phone him with the news. She would be better at doing it than I would.

I needed to ask Martha a few questions before the doctor arrived. I found her in the kitchen with her large feet up on the table. She was reading an old detective story and listening to country music on the radio. I turned it off.

"Hey! What did you do that for?" she asked.

"Martha," I said. "We've got to talk."

"What about?"

"What do you think? Mrs. Whittaker, of course. When did you last see Mrs. Whittaker alive?" I asked.

"When I took in her hot chocolate," Martha said. "Ten o'clock last night."

"Do you normally give Mrs. Whittaker her pills?"

"Sure I do. Two at bedtime to help her sleep," Martha replied.

"And was last night like every other night?" I asked.

"Yeah, why shouldn't it be?" she said. "Why are you

asking me all these questions?"

"It's my job. When did you find her this morning?"

"Same time as usual," Martha replied.

"Yes," I said patiently, "but what time is that?"

"Eight fifteen. There she was. Cold."

I looked around the kitchen. "You haven't touched anything in her room?"

"No sir," said Martha, waving her book at me. "I know that from detective stories. Never touch a thing."

But she had. The hot chocolate cup had been washed. I knew something was wrong. Martha was cheerful. She seemed to be enjoying every moment. The doctor had arrived before I could worry anymore. Stella showed him in.

"Nat, this is Dr. Hughes," she said.

"Pleased to meet you," I said. "The name's Marley. I'm working for Mrs. Whittaker. Martha called me with the news."

The doctor went into the bedroom and did an examination to establish how Mrs. Whittaker had died. After a few minutes, I knocked on the door and joined him in the bedroom. The doctor had covered her with a sheet.

"To be honest, Mr. Marley, I've been expecting this," the doctor said. "She's had a heart condition for some time. A natural death. I'll make out a death certificate now. Has the family been told yet?"

"I've just been talking to the son," replied Stella. "Charlie Whittaker's on his way."

"Good. Now the body must be moved to a funeral home as quickly as possible. Obviously the family will make those arrangements," said Dr. Hughes.

I felt uncomfortable about the whole situation. Something wasn't right, but I couldn't say exactly what. Martha was standing close, listening to every word. I had to get rid of her for a while.

"Martha, coffee for everybody. And I always have chocolate chip cookies with my morning coffee," I said.

"We don't have them," said Martha.

"Here's five dollars. Go and get some, will you?"

Dr. Hughes and Stella looked surprised as Martha left.

"That should take her ten minutes," I said.

"Nat, why are you sending Martha shopping?" asked Stella.

"Martha's far too cheerful for my liking," I said. "And I don't want her listening in to every word the doctor says. She's acting strange. It makes me nervous when she smiles. Did Mrs. Whittaker take sleeping pills regularly, Doctor?"

"Yes. I suggested she take them," the doctor replied. "She'd been having trouble sleeping."

"Could you take a look at the bottle?" I asked.

I went into the bedroom with the doctor.

"That seems to be about the right number," he said. "She has a fresh bottle every month. Now, Mr. Marley, surely you don't think ...?"

"I don't know what to think, Doctor. That's the problem," I said.

"Look, Mr. Marley," Dr. Hughes said, "Mrs. Whittaker was an old lady with a heart problem. Her death is no surprise. Well, there you are, one death certificate. Not much more I can do here. Is someone going to wait here with Martha?"

"I'll do that, Doctor," I said. "And thanks."

I didn't feel I should leave Martha alone with the body. While I was waiting, there was work that Stella could do.

"There's no point in the two of us staying here," I said to Stella. "Could you go back to the office and call those cab companies? We've got to find Jackie, and soon."

Later, Martha returned with the cookies. She gave

me one of her black looks.

"Mmm! My favorite," I said. "When you've made that coffee, come and sit down and tell me all about yourself."

That was pointless. I don't think even Captain Oldenberg would have been successful getting information out of her. The most I got out of her was a simple "Yes," "No," or "Don't know." Anyway, it helped to pass the time while I was waiting for Charlie to turn up. I really wanted to be out on the street looking for Jackie.

Chapter 9
The lost son found

Charlie Whittaker arrived at the Century Apartments in the early afternoon. Without intending to, I gave him an unpleasant surprise.

"My God! You frightened the life out of me! So you're Nat Marley?" he said with an amazed look on his face. "You could be my father's ghost. That brings back some bad memories. The way he used to check my homework. He always hit me if I got less than eight out of ten."

"Then I hope appearance is the only thing I share with your father," I said. "I'm sorry about your mother, Mr. Whittaker."

"Thanks," Charlie said sadly, "but we were sort of expecting it."

I sent Martha into the kitchen to make more coffee, and showed Charlie into the bedroom. He pulled back the sheet and stood there looking thoughtfully.

"Well, goodbye Mom," he said finally.

"I know this is not a good time, but could we talk?" I asked. "Wilma Patterson has explained the situation about the will. I wish to say that I never agreed with it. Wilma has my instructions to give everything to the family – money, apartment and so on. I'll just need to sign the papers," I said.

"Thanks. It's not your fault you were caught up in this."

"I'm worried about Martha," I said. "Her behavior's very strange."

"I can't remember a time when her behavior wasn't strange," Charlie said. "You don't have to stay. I can see to everything here now."

"Here's my card. If there's anything I can do, call me."

The Whittaker family had taken up a lot of valuable time. Something we didn't have much of. Back at East 43rd Street, Stella was still calling all the cab companies.

"Oh, hi there. Wonder if you could help me? You don't have a driver named Jackie Clayton working for you, huh? No? Thanks anyway."

She put the phone down.

"Nat," she said, "that makes cab company number

fifty. We'll get there eventually."

"Good work, Stella. And if you have to, call Staten Island and Brooklyn too."

Before she could continue, the phone rang. Someone was shouting at the other end. Stella held the phone at arm's length. It was Captain Oldenberg.

"Oldenberg, how are things?" I asked.

"I've been trying to get through to you all morning. Your phone's been busy all the time," Oldenberg replied in his usual direct way. "Thanks for the information about Wiseman. My boys searched his place and you should see the stuff we found there. He's going to jail for a long time."

"Look, Oldenberg, I need to speak to Wiseman."

I explained how we needed to find Jackie Clayton so he could see his dying mother.

"Sure you can speak to him. But will he speak to you?" asked the Captain.

Downtown on the number four express train, I was at Police Plaza quicker than any cab could make it through Manhattan. Captain Oldenberg was expecting me at Police Headquarters, and took me down to the cells. It brought back memories of my years with the NYPD. Wiseman was his usual sweet self. Physically, he seemed to be in worse shape than Mrs. Whittaker.

"Mr. Wiseman, you remember me? Nat Marley, private investigator. I need your help. I've got to find Jackie Clayton before his mother dies."

"If I could get my hands on him, I'd tear him into little pieces," replied Wiseman.

"Very thoughtful, I'm sure, but that doesn't help me."

"Me and Jackie were partners. Then he left me and broke our agreement. We had an understanding. He won't get anywhere without me. Leave me alone. I don't talk to private eyes. Guys like you make me sick."

At least I'd learned something. Jackie was trying to escape from his past. Maybe when we caught up with him, he'd agree to see his mother. It was now mid-afternoon. I phoned Stella to see how she was doing with the cabs.

"Nat?" she said. "We got something. Patel Cabs on West 14th. I even got to speak to him. But he just said 'I don't have any ex-girlfriends' and put the phone down."

"This is a job for Joe Blaney," I said. "Get him to watch the place. Can you give me the address?"

"Ninth and 14th," Stella said. "You know, where all

the meatpacking places are."

"Right. And tell Joe I'll see him there."

By the time I got there, Joe was already in position. Sitting in his car with his hat pulled down over his eyes, he looked just like a guy sleeping. But I knew he was paying attention to every little movement on that street. Late afternoon. The meat packers had stopped work for the day. We were parked under an old railroad bridge between two huge trucks. Patel Cabs was on the other side of the street a little further up. This could take a long time. We watched and waited. Cabs came and went but no sign of Jackie. As the hours passed, we slowly cooked in the heat. Eventually, I saw him.

"There he is, Joe," I said.

Jackie had changed. This wasn't the hard guy in the newspaper picture. He just looked like any normal guy going about his normal business. I ran across the road and called, "Jackie Clayton! We've got to talk. It's about your mother."

He didn't stop to listen. As soon as I'd said "Jackie," he was running like a frightened man. And he was a lot faster than I was. We lost him in a narrow entrance between two factories. And of course, he knew the area better then we did. Not much more we could do there. Our last chance was to ask at Patel Cabs. The receptionist didn't like the look of us.

"Look," she said to us. "Jackie said if anyone comes around here asking questions, I'm to say nothing."

"Thanks ma'am," I said. "Message understood."

Eight in the evening. I was tired, hot, and hungry.

"Not much more we can do today, Joe."

I made a couple of calls on my cell phone. I told Stella to go home, and asked Dr. Fischer to give Annie a message. If Annie knew we'd seen Jackie, that might just help to keep her holding on to life.

We made our way across to Eighth Avenue. Three blocks uptown there was a Cuban-Chinese restaurant where they did great chicken and rice, and more importantly, ice-cold beer. It made me feel a little better, but I still felt useless.

"Joe, we were so close. Now Jackie will be nervous about any stranger he meets," I said.

"Nothing you could do, boss," said Joe.

"But we've still got one more chance. Oldenberg. We helped him out with Wiseman, so he owes us something. He could give us Jackie's address. The New York Taxi and Limousine Commission holds the records of every cab driver in this city. That information's private, but not to the NYPD."

I phoned Police Headquarters. Fortunately, Oldenberg was still in the building.

"Don't you have a home to go to, Oldenberg?" I asked.

"Marley, I've got teenage kids. Police Headquarters is more peaceful," he laughed.

"I gave you Wiseman so I think you owe me. I need the address of a cab driver. Name of Jackie Clayton. The one I told you about. Drives for Patel Cabs on West 14th. As soon as possible, Oldenberg. His mother's dying."

"I'll do what I can," he said. "But I can't promise anything until tomorrow. The office you need is closed now."

All we could do was wait.

Chapter 10
We're the good guys

I hate the way sweat makes your shirt stick to the train seats. I was going through three or four clean shirts a day in this heat. I needed a fresh shirt this morning, but there was no time to change. At the office, Charlie Whittaker and Wilma Patterson were waiting.

"Mr. Marley, thank God you're here!" said Charlie. "I'd like you to come with us to the apartment. I'll explain in the cab. Martha's disappeared."

"OK, let's go. Stella, call me at Century Apartments as soon as Oldenberg calls."

In the cab, Charlie Whittaker explained what had happened. "Mom's been taken to the funeral home. Mrs. Patterson and I agreed to meet at the apartment first thing this morning to start going through mom's papers. I checked into a hotel last night. I didn't like the idea of sleeping in that apartment. We got there at 7:30 AM to find the place in a real mess. There was stuff all over the floor. At first I thought it was a break-in, but Martha's room hadn't been touched. I thought that was strange."

"Is anything missing?" I asked.

"No idea, yet, Mr. Marley. That's where I hoped you would help. Can you find out what's been going on and find Martha? I just feel something is very wrong."

Inside the Whittaker apartment there were books and papers thrown everywhere, broken pieces of furniture and glass on the carpets. The sofas and armchairs had been cut all over and their insides pulled out. The kitchen floor was wet with oil, milk, and wine which was slowly mixing with bags of flour and sugar. A broken bottle of ketchup sat in the bath tub in a pool of shampoo. In the toilet were the torn-up pieces of the Whittakers' wedding photographs.

"Now take a look in Martha's room," said Charlie.

The small, simple bedroom was clean and tidy. There was no suitcase and it looked as if she had taken most of her things. The bookshelf was full of detective stories: Raymond Chandler, Ellery Queen, Ed McBain. On the mirror, she'd written in red lipstick: "Gone to play ball."

"What does the mystery message mean?" asked

Wilma.

"I'm not sure yet, but this is definitely Martha's work," I answered.

"What now?" asked Charlie.

"Find everything that hasn't been taken – money, checkbooks, credit cards. We need to find out what's missing. Don't make it look like you've been searching. We shouldn't really touch a thing until the police have been here."

"The police? Do we have to?" asked Charlie.

"Mr. Whittaker, murder is police business."

"Surely you don't think Martha ..."

"That's exactly what I think. I knew something was wrong all along."

"What do I say?" Charlie asked.

"Report a murder. They'll be here before you put the phone down. And Mr. Whittaker, before you call 911, call the funeral home now. Tell them not to touch your mother's body. If they're preparing it for the funeral, tell them to stop now. The police will have to look closely at your mother's body to find out how she died. There has to be an immediate autopsy."

We had time for a quick look around before the police arrived. No sign of checkbooks, cash, or credit cards. The NYPD team was at the apartment in under ten minutes.

A call came through from Stella.

"Nat? We got an address for Jackie. The Chelsea Arms Hotel. Near the corner of Eighth and 22nd."

"In Chelsea, huh? We went by there last night. This is what to do. Phone the hospital, get a message to Annie. Say we know where Jackie's living. Then see if Jackie's at work. Pretend you're from the Taxi and Limousine Commission. Say you want to speak to Mr. Clayton about a customer who's taken his number and complained about him. That way you should find out when he comes in to work or when he finishes. Call me back here."

Wilma came over with the lieutenant from the Crime-Scene Team.

"We've had a look around, sir," he said. "No sign yet of anything stolen. Mr. Whittaker, can you tell me where your mother kept cash, credit cards, that sort of thing?"

"Her handbag, probably," said Charlie.

The lieutenant turned to one of his men. "Sergeant, did you check that?"

"Nothing, Lieutenant. It was empty."

"Now Mr. Whittaker, do you know where your mother banked?" I asked.

"Chase Manhattan," Charlie answered.

"Would you call them now? We have to know what's happened to her bank account."

As Charlie was about to pick up the phone, it rang.

"It's for you, Mr. Marley," he said.

"Hi, Nat. It's me. I've made the call. Jackie may be at the hotel now," said Stella.

"Has Joe come in? Good. Tell him to wait for me outside the hotel. Now I've got an idea that just might work. Make me up a big, brown paper package. Fill it with old newspapers and magazines and give it to Joe."

"Sure," replied Stella.

Time was very short. I caught a downtown train to 23rd Street. As I came up to street level from the subway, I could see Joe waiting at the corner of Eighth and 22nd, with the package under his arm. He was pretending to read the *Daily News*.

The Chelsea Arms Hotel had seen better days. Now it just looked like any other cheap hotel. The floor was dirty white stone in the lobby. A guy was working on the computer, behind the window at the reception desk. There was another big guy sitting at a table opposite the reception desk. He was obviously there in case of any trouble.

"Joe, stay just outside the door on the street. Keep an eye out. If Jackie tries to run, stop him any way you can."

Now, I hoped this was going to work. I quickly wrote a message on the package and wandered over to reception.

"Is there a Mr. Jackie Clayton staying here?" I asked. "Package for him."

"You can leave it with me," said the receptionist.

"Sorry. Special package," I said. "Has to be signed for by Mr. Clayton."

"I'll call the room."

A minute later Jackie came down the stairs into the lobby, looking nervously from side to side. I waved the package at him.

"What's this?" he said. "I'm not expecting anything."

"Read it," I said. "It's for you."

Jackie took the package. The message read: "Jackie – your mother is dying and wants to see you. Time is short."

He wasn't sure what to do. I moved around to cut off the stairs. Jackie threw the package in my face and made a run for the front door, only to see Joe standing in his way. Then he tried to hit Joe. Not a good idea. Especially when the guy you're trying to hit is an ex-NYPD heavyweight boxer. Joe replied with his famous straight left. A loud cry of pain from Jackie. He fell backwards into my arms.

The big guy at the table stood up. "Stop that or I'll call 911!" he shouted.

I held my license in his face.

"Nathan Marley, private investigator," I said. "I've been hired by this guy's mother to find him." I turned to Jackie. "Listen, Jackie, your mom's seriously ill. We're the good guys. We're not from Wiseman. Your mother hired us to find you. You've got to believe us. Look, get reception to call Bellevue Hospital – then you'll believe us."

Jackie was calming down. He nodded to the guy at reception who called the hospital and then passed the phone to Jackie. Jackie spoke slowly and quietly. "Do you have a patient there by the name of Annie Clayton? ... You do? ... I'll be right over." Jackie put the phone down, turned around, and took our hands. "Guys," he said, "I owe you an apology. I thought you were more unwelcome guests. Let's move. I haven't seen my mom in twenty years."

Chapter 11
Martha Bianchi

The hospital was more or less directly east across town. A cab was the best idea and we found one on Eighth Avenue.

"Driver, Bellevue Hospital," I said.

On the way, I told Jackie his mother's story.

"So mom's been on the street all this time?" he asked.

"Ever since she last saw you – in a cell," I said.

"I thought I knew everything," he said. "Thought I was hard and tough and didn't need anybody. Now I know better. Families are part of you. I used to think Wiseman and the boys were family. But they weren't any more family than the driver here. As long as you were doing your job OK, it was cool. But one mistake and you were out."

"What was your mistake, Jackie?" I asked.

"I wanted a normal life. I was tired of looking over my shoulder for cops. I wanted an ordinary job and a place I could call my own. Then I started thinking of my family. Hey, are we going to be in time?"

"We'll make it OK," I replied.

"Wiseman hates it when people try to leave the organization," Jackie continued. "The last twelve months I've been trying to earn a living and hide from him at the same time. It was almost impossible to do both. I tried to find mom and went back to the Bronx, where I grew up. Everything's changed. Didn't even recognize my own street. All the old housing projects pulled down. Nobody had heard of Annie Clayton."

We stopped outside the hospital. The driver had earned his twenty-dollar tip. The clerk at reception phoned Dr. Fischer, who came down immediately to meet Jackie.

"Jackie Clayton, the long lost son. You're going to make your mother a very happy woman," she said.

"How is she, doctor?" asked Jackie.

"To be honest, she doesn't have long to live. She hasn't got the strength. All those years on the street. But she's holding on for you. Take it easy when you go in. She gets tired very easily. We'll go right up," said the doctor.

Jackie turned to me. "Nat, will you come in with me?"

"Sure," I said.

Annie was asleep, her mouth open. The doctor

shook her arm gently. “Annie, he’s come back,” said the doctor.

The tiredness disappeared from her face. A wide smile. Tears in her eyes. Jackie took her hand.

“Why! If it isn’t my big stupid son come back to see his mom after all these years,” she whispered.

“Sorry, Mom. I was a no-good kid. I’ve changed. I’ve been trying to find you.”

“Come here. Let me hold you tight. That’s better.”

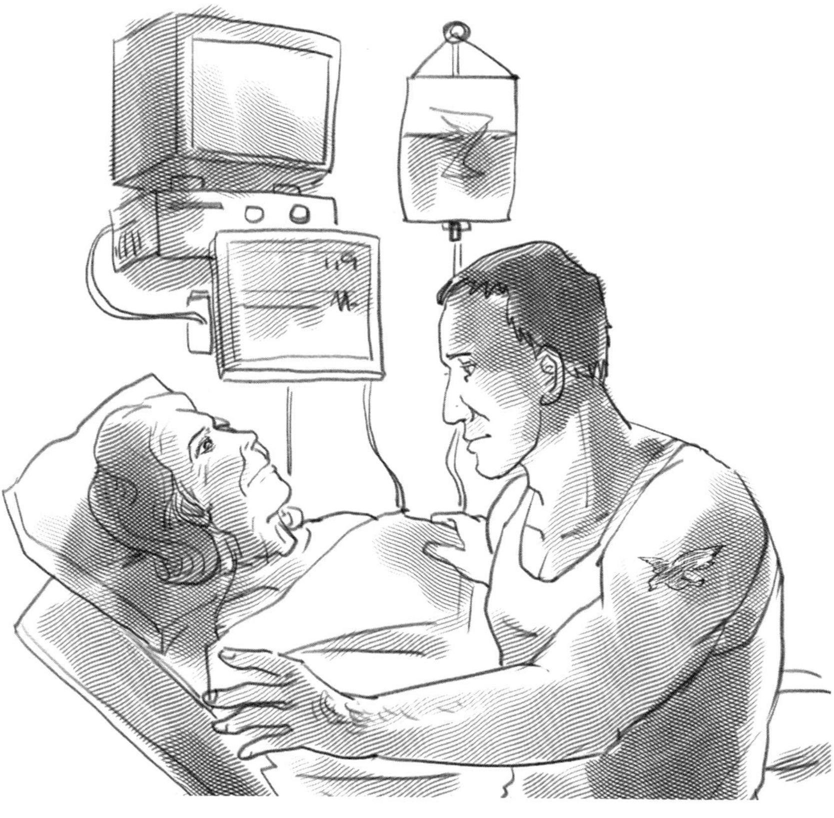

"Mom, this guy Nat's amazing. He didn't give up."

Annie turned to me and smiled. Underneath the smile, she was exhausted.

"Nat, I don't know how to thank you," she said softly.

They needed to be alone together. My day wasn't finished, though. I called Stella at East 43rd Street.

"Nat, how's it going?" she asked.

"We found Jackie," I said. "Joe persuaded him to listen. He's with Annie now. The doctor doesn't expect her to live much longer."

"Poor woman," Stella said.

"Stella, you've done more than enough for one week. You found Jackie. Close the office and enjoy your weekend. I'm going back to the Whittaker apartment with Joe."

I wouldn't have minded a weekend off myself. The effects of the heat and tiredness were beginning to hit me. There was a line of cabs outside the hospital. Joe and I jumped in the first one.

The traffic was heavy, but the delay gave me time to think. What was in Mrs. Whittaker's bedtime drink? Could the autopsy establish it was the drink that killed Mrs. Whittaker? If Martha had the strength to destroy furniture, she would easily be able to murder Mrs. Whittaker. But how? She appeared to have died peacefully and the doctor didn't seem to think there was anything unusual about the death. The cab was now standing still in the traffic. An opportunity to get some sleep.

Joe shook me awake at the Century Apartments. In the apartment, the Crime-Scene Team was getting ready to leave. Charlie Whittaker and Wilma Patterson were checking through papers. Some were wet and dirty. I didn't want to think what Martha had poured over them.

"Any news from the funeral home?" I asked the lieutenant.

"We were lucky, sir," he said. "They hadn't prepared Mrs. Whittaker for the funeral and there'll be an autopsy this evening. Not much more we can do here."

Charlie Whittaker turned to me. "Guess what," he said. "The lieutenant interviewed all the neighbors. They all heard some noise during the night, when Martha destroyed the furniture. They thought it was a wild party. Since when did my mother have wild parties?"

"Would have been some party," I laughed.

"There's nothing wrong with the locks," Charlie went on. "No break-in. It all looks like Martha's work, Mr. Marley. Most of my mother's papers are here. Ugh! There's ketchup on this one. But no checkbook or credit cards. I phoned the bank and luckily there was someone there who could help. I had to go over there myself. The bank account's overdrawn. It looks like Martha's taken out tens of thousands of dollars."

"Spending it on what, I wonder," I said.

"Mr. Marley, find that woman, and quick," Charlie said. "I want her to pay for what she's done."

"We're on the job, Mr. Whittaker. First, we need to go through everything in Martha's room."

The message "Gone to play ball" was still on the mirror.

"What sort of 'ball' might that be, boss?" asked Joe.

"Was Martha a baseball fan?" I asked. "The answer's got to be in here somewhere. We can start by going through these books."

There was a shelf full of old detective stories which looked as if they had been read again and again. That only told us she liked reading. Then Joe found a book open on the floor by the bed.

"Look at this book, boss," Joe said. "Martha's been

marking parts of it."

The book was called *The Perfect Murder*. The pages were yellow with age.

I looked through the book, reading what Martha had underlined. One sentence especially caught my eye:

"She kicked a bit when I put the pillow over her face. But it was soon all over. If killing is so easy, why not do it again? They say 'practice makes perfect.'"

I showed it to Joe.

"I think Martha reads too much," he said. Joe pointed at the inside cover of another book. "Look. She's been practicing how to sign Mrs. Whittaker's name."

I showed the book to Charlie Whittaker.

"Is this how your mother signs her name?" I asked.

"That's it. That's how Martha managed to get the money out of mom's bank account."

We went back to our work in Martha's room. No suitcase, no handbag. Her own things were missing. We then started on the pile of vacation booklets that Joe had found under the bed. Las Vegas, Oneida, and Atlantic City.

"There's only one sort of ball you can play at these

places," I said to Joe. " And that's in a casino."

Martha could now be losing all Mrs. Whittaker's money at a casino. We didn't know where she had gone and there was no way we could phone a casino and ask, "Do you have anyone at the gambling tables matching the following description ...?" Even if a casino did agree to help, there could be any number of middle-aged women losing their money. The type of people who save up all year for a week's gambling vacation. They spend every cent and go home poor.

"Where do you think she's gone?" I asked Joe.

"My guess is nearer rather than further," he replied.

"Atlantic City is the closest," I said. "Do you know how many casinos there are in Atlantic City? At least ten, maybe more."

There was hardly anything in the room that told you Martha had a life of her own. We had searched everywhere for a photo of her. Nothing to show to people. Our only course of action was to visit each casino until we found her.

"So what now, boss?" asked Joe.

"Atlantic City's several hours' drive away," I said. "We may need to spend all day there. Bring your car to the office, nine o'clock tomorrow. And make sure you get some rest."

I paused for a moment. I'd just had a thought.

"Joe, isn't this all a bit too obvious? If Martha really wanted to disappear, why write that message and leave the books? Somehow, I think she wants us to find her. As if she's acting out one of those detective stories. But who knows?"

It seemed to be hotter than ever. I'd had enough. When was this weather going to break? It was going to be another long day tomorrow and I'd lost my weekend. I had some bedtime reading to do – *The Perfect Murder*.

Chapter 12
Atlantic City

I had stayed awake reading most of the night. Not by choice – I just couldn't sleep in the heat. At sunrise I gave up and got dressed. Outside it was almost pleasant. That wouldn't last long. There was time to stop by Bellevue Hospital. I knew it would be too early to visit Annie, but maybe the nurse would be able to tell me the latest on Annie's condition.

At the hospital, the nurse took me to the door of Annie's room and raised her finger to her lips.

"Not a sound," she whispered. "Just look at this."

Annie Clayton and her son Jackie were both asleep. Jackie was sitting beside the bed with his head on the pillow. Annie's hand was in Jackie's.

"He hasn't left her all this time," said the nurse.

"What about Annie?" I asked.

She led me away from the room. She looked serious. I was expecting the worst.

"There's nothing more we can do," the nurse said. "It's just a question of waiting. It could be today or tomorrow."

"I'm sorry," I said. "Call me if there are any developments."

At East 43rd Street, I called Police Headquarters to check if there were any results from the autopsy on Mrs. Whittaker. The news didn't make me feel any better.

"They say she died of a heart attack. If it's a natural death, then there's nothing more to do."

"What about the results of the drug tests?" I asked.

"It's too early. Tomorrow, maybe."

The problem was how to make the NYPD believe it was murder. If the drug tests showed there was a normal level of the drug in her body, we couldn't show that Martha murdered her – unless she admitted it.

Joe arrived at the office bright and fresh. Me, I couldn't stop yawning.

"Why are you so cheerful?" I asked him on the way to his car.

"I got a good night's sleep, boss, just like you suggested," Joe replied.

"Well, I'm exhausted. Wake me up in Atlantic City."

I stretched out on the back seat and soon fell asleep. The best sleep I'd had for days. Several hours later, Joe woke me as we were entering the city, along the

Atlantic City Expressway.

"You've been sleeping like a baby, boss," he said.

Unlike the city, the casinos were beautiful buildings in every possible design and color. We parked and walked along beside the ocean, and started looking inside the casinos. It was the same story in each one. Lonely people kissing goodbye to good money. But no sign of Martha. We had visited five casinos by the time we arrived at the Golden Palace.

"I don't believe it, boss!" Joe said. "I've never seen anything like it."

On our way in, we passed a line of large, white stone elephants. Inside it was a dream world. The lights above were clouds of brilliant stars. Soft music was playing. Dark wood, deep carpets, shining gold and silver everywhere. Early afternoon, and people were crowded around the roulette tables.

"Over there, Joe! It's Martha."

There she was, sitting between two old ladies. Martha made them look tiny. In front of her, Martha had piles of brightly colored casino chips. She was playing for big money and had placed chips on numbers 7, 14, 21, and 28. The ball shot around and around and finally landed on 7. Martha screamed with laughter.

"It's me again!" she shouted. "That's the way to do it. I knew I couldn't lose!"

I couldn't watch her any longer. I went up to her.

"Martha," I said. "We've got to talk."

"Well, if it isn't Mister Private Eye himself," she answered. "I wondered when you'd get here. Leave me alone. I'm winning."

She started placing more chips on the table. That was enough. I pushed them onto the floor.

"Hey, what do you think you're doing?" she shouted.

"Excuse me," said a voice behind me. "Is there a problem here?" There was a heavy hand on my shoulder. I turned around. A tall, powerful guy in a black suit, wearing his casino ID on his jacket.

"Leave this lady alone and get out before I call the police," he said.

I held up my investigator's license. Now I had to move fast. Everything depended on Martha admitting to murder.

"Nat Marley, private investigator," I said. "This lady is using stolen money. Money she stole from her employer, who she murdered. Didn't you, Martha? We know everything about the money and the pills. Just like it said in that detective story you like so much."

There was total silence around the roulette table. People stared at us with open mouths. I held up Martha's book.

"Aren't you the clever one!" said Martha. "I was wondering how long it would take you. Faster than I expected. Sure I got the idea from the book. Couple of extra sleeping pills in her hot chocolate. Then it was no more 'Martha do this, Martha do that!' Just put a pillow over her head. She kicked a bit, but it was all over in seconds. Easy. And her face looked perfect. Everything happened just like the book said it would. Only quicker and easier. It was her own fault. She left me out of the will!"

"You read too much," I said.

The man in the suit was beginning to understand.

"You'd better come to the office," he said. "Do you want to call the police, Mr. Marley?"

"With pleasure," I said. "And would you collect all those chips. That's stolen money."

It was another couple of hours before we were finished at the Atlantic City Police Headquarters. Martha admitted everything again to the New Jersey police. She wasn't sorry at all. In fact, she seemed to be enjoying it.

"What now, Lieutenant?" Martha asked. "You going to lock me up in a cell?"

"Yes. Until the NYPD comes to get you," the lieutenant replied. "Sergeant, take her away. Now, Mr. Marley, I'll speak to Captain Oldenberg. This is NYPD business."

It was late afternoon. We had to get back to New York. I could make some calls on the way. I'd been thinking about Annie all day. I managed to get through to Dr. Fischer at Bellevue. She didn't expect Annie to last the night and Jackie had been asking for me. There was no time to lose.

Another call, to Charlie Whittaker who was waiting to hear from us. Luckily, he was still at the Century Apartments.

"Mr. Whittaker?" I said. "We found Martha. In Atlantic City."

"You did? She murdered my mother?" asked Charlie.

"She admitted everything," I told him. "It was just like I thought. She was gambling at the casino like she was a millionaire."

"The money's not important," Charlie said. "I want her to pay for what she's done."

"Don't worry. She will."

It was dark by the time we reached the hospital. Jackie was waiting for us outside Annie's room.

"You guys are great, all you've done for us," said Jackie.

"Don't mention it. How's Annie?" I asked.

"Mom's going slowly. She's unconscious now. She managed to talk about old times. At least she's not in pain."

"We'll stay with you, Jackie. At a time like this you need friends around you. I've known your mother for a long time. I want to be there when she leaves us."

Jackie went back inside. We waited until early morning, watching the hands of the clock move around and around. A hospital is a very strange place at that time of night. The dying waiting, hour after hour, for the moment of death. At 2:30 AM, the nurse called Dr. Fischer. After a quick examination, she waved to us to come in. Annie's breathing was now slow and irregular. Finally, it came to a stop. Jackie was still holding his mother's hand.

"I'm sorry, Jackie. She's gone," the doctor said.

Jackie looked up at us. “She never gave up hope for me,” he said. “Could you leave me alone with mom for a minute?”

Outside, Joe looked at me closely.

“Nat! You’ve got tears in your eyes,” he said.

“Tears? Me? No, must have got something in my eye.”

He was right though. Annie’s death had affected me deeply. More than I had imagined it would. But I hadn’t felt a thing when Mrs. Whittaker died. Ten minutes later, Jackie came out.

“Let’s get you home, Jackie,” I said sadly. “I’m going to miss those morning chats with Annie at Grand Central.”

Chapter 13
Rain

Another Monday morning. When I walked out of Grand Central to 42nd Street, the sky was heavy with black storm clouds. You could almost feel the electricity in the air. At last the weather was going to change. As I got to the office, fat raindrops were starting to hit the sidewalk.

Stella was at her desk as usual.

"Nat, there's a visitor," she said.

"Who?" I asked.

"Go and see."

"Why the mystery?"

The sky was suddenly lit up. Then darkness and a crash of thunder. Inside the office was a face I knew only too well. Another crash of thunder. Pouring rain. The storm had started.

"Oldenberg! You sure know how to frighten a guy."

"I love this, Marley," Oldenberg said. "Did you know there's always less crime during bad weather?"

"You're not here to talk about the weather. Why *are* you here?"

Oldenberg wanted to speak to Jackie Clayton. He needed his help to put Wiseman in jail. In return, the police had promised Jackie a new life with a clean record. Jackie trusted me so I was asked to set up the meeting.

After Oldenberg left, the storm got worse. Rivers of rainwater in the streets. And more visitors. Stella showed in two workmen.

"Nat, a pleasant surprise this time," Stella said.

"Mr. Marley, we've come to put in the air conditioning," said one of the workmen.

"I don't believe it. Why weren't you here last week?" I asked.

The crashes and bangs as they started putting in the units made it almost impossible to work. Maybe I should move somewhere with a better climate. Like Alaska. Who needs air conditioning in Anchorage? It wasn't the best time to get another visitor. It was Wilma Patterson. She wanted me to arrange a meeting with Jackie at her office tomorrow morning to read his mother's will. Then the phone rang. More crashing and banging from the workmen.

"Can you guys stop that for just a minute?" I asked. "Marley here. Sorry about that."

"It's Charlie Whittaker. I need your advice. I've been speaking to Captain Oldenberg. The police aren't sure if Martha can be tried for murder."

"Go on," I said.

"There's no problem with the money," Charlie said. "The checkbook and credit cards were in her handbag. She definitely stole it all. But as for murder. The woman's crazy. She seems to be living in a dream world of detective stories. No one can say if she's telling the truth or telling another story. The autopsy results don't help us either. Nothing definite from the results of the drug test so it's still a natural death. What do you advise, Nat?"

"She'll go to jail for a long time for stealing the money and what she did to the apartment," I said. "She knew exactly what she was doing when she emptied your mother's bank account. It's a difficult one, Mr. Whittaker. It looks as if she'll be tried for stealing, not murder. But either way, she'll be in jail for a long time. And life in a New York State jail is no picnic. I'd accept what Oldenberg says. You know and I know she's guilty of murder. But getting people to believe it is another matter."

"Well, that's not what I wanted to hear," said

Charlie. “But I don’t suppose there’s much we can do about it now. Anyway, if she isn’t tried for murder, they can return mom’s body sooner for the funeral.”

Another call. This time it was Jackie, to tell me that Annie’s funeral was going to be at 11:00 AM on Saturday morning in Queens. I promised to be there. Jackie said he could make it to Wilma’s office at ten o’clock tomorrow to hear his mother’s will. I wasn’t sure how he was going to take Oldenberg’s suggestion.

“One more thing, Jackie,” I said. “I know it’s not a good time, but Captain Oldenberg wants to see you.”

“I don’t like the sound of this, Nat,” Jackie said.

“Just hold on, Jackie. They want to get Wiseman, but they need dates, times, names, places, and so on. In return, they’ll forget about anything you might have done for Wiseman in the past. This could be the fresh start you need.”

“That’s a lot to think about, Nat,” Jackie said. “I’ll tell you tomorrow.”

With all the noise in the office it was impossible to work. “We’re going to take a long lunch break,” I shouted to the workmen. “There are the keys. If you finish before we’re back, leave them in the lobby. If those units don’t work ...”

"Trust us, mister," said one of the workmen. "We could do this in our sleep."

The long lunch break lasted most of the afternoon. I was feeling increasingly tired after all the action last week. I left Stella to lock up the office and escaped back to Queens to get some sleep.

The next morning, midtown Manhattan smelled fresh and clean after the storms. A cloudless blue sky. Was it going to be another hot one? Then I remembered. I'd paid seven hundred dollars for air conditioning. Those units had better work. As I stepped inside the office at East 43rd Street, I could feel ice in the air.

"What's this?" I asked. "Siberia?"

"Sorry, Nat," said Stella. "Just having a little trouble with the air conditioning."

"Well, I'd rather fry than freeze."

"Come on, Nat! I'm doing my best. I can't always be right. I'm just a human being, not superwoman. Oh, by the way, Wilma Patterson phoned. Could you be at her office by nine thirty?"

At Wilma's office, there was a pile of papers for me to sign. Everything that Mrs. Whittaker had left to me would now go to Charlie Whittaker and his sister Betty

Osborne, in equal shares. Just the way it should have happened in the first place.

"Nat, there's the question of your fee," said Wilma.

"I'll get Stella to send Mr. Whittaker my bill," I said.

"That won't be necessary," she said. "He told me to give you this. He hopes it's enough." She handed me an envelope full of money.

It was more than enough. Very kind. Now I wouldn't feel so bad about the air conditioning. By ten o'clock, Jackie, Wilma, Stella, and I were sitting around Annie's metal box. Wilma took the key and unlocked it.

"Mr. Clayton," she said, "your mother's will is very simple. Everything in this box is yours to use as you wish."

Inside was a pile of papers. On top lay an envelope with the words "For my son, Jackie." Jackie opened it and read the letter aloud.

To my darling son, Jackie,

I don't know where you are but I've been keeping this for you all these years. A present from the daddy you never knew. He was a big businessman. If what's here is worth anything, use it to give yourself a future.

Your loving mom

"All that time she remembered me," said Jackie. "But

what are all these papers? And what does this note mean?"

Wilma took the papers and note from Jackie and looked through them.

"Mr. Clayton, this note must be from your father. Listen:

Annie, I can never be a real father to the child. Here's some money to help with food and clothes. And something for the future. Keep these stock certificates. One day they might be worth a lot of money.

Yours,

Tom"

"Who's this Tom?" asked Jackie.

"The answer must be here somewhere," said Wilma. She searched through the papers until she found the stock certificates. "Your mother has taken good care of you. See these certificates? This stock could be worth tens of thousands. Everything's been done properly. The stock is in your mother's name and they were given to her by ... I don't believe it: Tom Whittaker!"

"What's going on?" asked Jackie.

"Jackie, I think I know who your father was. I remember Annie telling me she had once worked as an office cleaner, where she met the top man in the company. That man was Tom Whittaker. A big businessman, president of Whittaker Air."

In my wallet, I still had the photocopy of the *Daily News* story with Tom Whittaker's picture.

"That's him, Jackie. Keep it. And that's not all, Jackie. You've got family. A half-brother and half-sister. Charlie Whittaker and Betty Osborne. They live upstate."

Jackie was silent for a while, then he turned to Wilma.

"Mrs. Patterson, there's something I have to know. It's important. What would have happened if mom had died without seeing me? Or I had refused to see her, or if Nat never found me, or if I had died. If, if, if ..."

"Just in case anything like that happened, Annie added an extra part to the will," Wilma explained. "The money from the sale of the stock would have gone to help homeless women. I don't think Annie had any real idea of its value."

"Mrs. Patterson, could you keep the stock certificates here for me?" Jackie asked. "I need time to think."

There were more things in the box. Some black and white family photographs. A young mother with a happy, smiling baby in her arms. Class photographs from an elementary school. Childhood birthday parties. Family days out on Coney Island. Now they were in color. An active, young teenager holding a baseball bat. Jackie's eyes were shining as he looked through the photos. The poor guy had gone through so much in the last few days. Lost his mother and found a family. A guy with no future now had hope. We sat in silence as Jackie discovered his childhood again. A few minutes later he was ready to speak. Now, he looked calm and confident.

"Nat, Mrs. Patterson," Jackie began. "My mind is made up. Mrs. Patterson, will you find out what this stock is worth? There's mom's hospital bills to pay, and Nat needs to be paid for all his work."

"Certainly," said Wilma.

"And Nat. You said I've got a half-brother and half-sister. I'd really like to meet them. They're family. You know the Whittakers, so would you arrange a meeting? And one more thing. I've been thinking about what you said yesterday. The answer's 'Yes.' I've got to do it if I want to make a clean break from my past. Call Captain Oldenberg. I'll do anything he wants if it's going to get Wiseman off my back and in a prison cell."

"Leave it to me, Jackie. We'll see you at the funeral."

Chapter 14

The Annie Clayton Center

There were no more than ten people at Annie's funeral, including Annie's friends Ellie and Leona, and Charlie Whittaker and Betty Osborne. I introduced Jackie to Charlie and Betty. They were still talking together when I left.

Mrs. Whittaker had a grand funeral a day or so later in Albany, with family and a few old drinking partners of Tom Whittaker. I had gone because I thought I should, not out of choice. The surprise was again seeing Jackie Clayton with Charlie and Betty. Maybe he had found his family.

Life had been quieter since mid-July. I had even taken a vacation. After that, I just got on with the usual daily work - divorce or looking for missing persons. Nothing exciting, but I wasn't complaining. I preferred it that way. Toward the end of September a letter arrived from a New York State prison. It was from Martha, but it looked like a child's handwriting.

To Mr. Nat Marley, the Private Eye,

I've had more fun in the last two months than I've had in the last twenty years. I like it fine here in jail. Everyone looks after me. Makes for a change. Nice people. I get along real well with my cellmate. She's inside for murder.

Martha

So Martha enjoyed life in jail. Life behind bars must suit her character. With her size and strength, she probably wouldn't get any trouble from the other prisoners. From her letter it sounded like they were good to her – better than Mrs. Whittaker had ever been. Anyway, society was safe from Martha Bianchi.

At last the heat of the summer was over, and I was enjoying my favorite season, fall. The trees in Central Park had turned into a sea of red and gold. Life in the office continued as normal. Fall turned into winter. In the office, Stella complained as much about the cold as she had about the heat the summer before. We were both glad when spring arrived.

It was one morning in spring that I found a surprise invitation in my mail. It was for the opening of the Annie Clayton Center on 125th Street. Stella and I could hardly believe it. So Jackie had found a way to give his mom something back after all.

On the morning of the opening, Stella, Joe and I traveled uptown to Harlem together. Outside the center was a group of important-looking people. Community leaders and local politicians. Reporters from newspapers and local TV stations. At the front door stood Jackie Clayton, Charlie Whittaker, and Betty Osborne.

Charlie Whittaker spoke first.

"Ladies and Gentlemen, I'd like to welcome you to the opening of the Annie Clayton Center. A building that will provide comfortable rooms for the homeless women of this city. Everyone will be welcome, no matter what her color or religion. The women who use this center will have one thing in common – nowhere to live. My sister and I, and my half-brother Jackie Clayton have all lost mothers recently. This building is in their memory."

Then Jackie stepped forward. He had changed since I had seen him last. This wasn't the frightened cab driver I had met in July. He looked and sounded confident as he spoke.

ANNIE CLAYTON CENTER

"Thank you, Charlie. My mother, Annie Clayton, lived on the streets of this city for over twenty years. She needed love and care, and as a young man, I refused her that love and care. If there had been a center like this, perhaps she could have been saved from the city streets. I sincerely hope that this center will provide for women like my mother for many years to come."

Charlie and Betty then joined Jackie. Betty spoke.

"Finally, we'd all like to say a special thank you to the man whose hard work made this all possible. Without him, we might never have met. An old friend of Annie Clayton's, Mr. Nat Marley."

She pointed toward me. Television cameras turned at the same time. Interviews with reporters followed. I had my photograph taken with Jackie and the Whittakers for the newspapers. It would be a great human interest story. Finally we were able to escape. Jackie took us into an office.

"We all owe you and your partners a big thank you for all you've done," said Jackie. "After the funerals, Charlie, Betty, and I got to talking and found we had a lot in common."

"Strange. The Bronx meets the Upper West Side,"

I said.

"You see, we've all lost mothers. And in different ways, we've had difficult childhoods. I was always getting into trouble on the street," said Jackie.

"And we had a cold, unloving father," said Charlie. "I still remember what it felt like growing up in that apartment. The things he used to do to mom."

"It was when I met Ellie and Leona, mom's old friends, that I started thinking," said Jackie. "Some way of using mom's money to help people like them. I talked it over with Charlie and Betty."

"The apartment was ours, but after everything that had happened, we never wanted to set foot in there again," said Charlie. "I felt we had to do something. Jackie's idea was to put our money together to do something to help improve people's lives. It's been a lot of hard work, but all worth it."

"What more can I say? This place is a great achievement," I said. "Annie was right never to lose hope in you, Jackie."

Finally we said our goodbyes. I started thinking as we walked along 125th Street in the sunshine. I'd said before that I'd seen the best and worst of life in this city. I was wrong. This center was the best I had ever seen. I still had mixed feelings, though. Annie had lived on the streets of New York while she'd had enough money for a place to live. She'd suffered when she didn't have to.

Stella touched my hand.

"You feeling all right, Nat?" she asked.

"Just thinking. The Annie Clayton Center. Something to remember her by. Almost like she has life after death. If only she'd known the value of that stock. She could have enjoyed life before death."

"She never had her fair share of what life can offer. But others will, Nat, others will."

After reading

读后活动

1. Would you like to live and work in a city like New York? Explain your answer.

2. Look at page 50. Marley felt, "Sad for the people who had to live out their lives on the streets. Angry about the society that put them on the streets." What do you think about homeless people?

3. Make two lists of the characters: 1) characters from the "high life," 2) characters from the "low life." Which characters do you like best or least from the two lists?

4. Look at page 104. Write Marley's reply to Martha's letter from jail.

5. Look at page 107. "Television cameras turned at the same time. Interviews with reporters followed." Imagine you are a TV reporter. What questions would you ask Marley?

6. Marley's team includes Stella Delgado and Joe Blaney. How did Stella and Joe help Marley in the investigation?

7. Imagine you are making a movie of *High Life, Low Life*. Which actors would you choose to play the characters? Would you change anything in the story?

8. Imagine you are a *Daily News* reporter. Finish the news story beginning on page 13.

9. Make your own activities for other students to do, e.g. write some "Who said what?" questions.

Learning guide | 学习指导

Chapter 1

New words 生词

- boiling /ˈbɔɪlɪŋ/ *a.* 很热的，滚热的
- character /ˈkærəktər/ *n.* 人物
- divorce /dɪˈvɔːrs/ *n.* 离婚
- downtown /ˌdaʊnˈtaʊn/ *ad.* 在市中心，往市中心
- eventually /ɪˈventʃuəli/ *ad.* 最终，终于
- exhausted /ɪɡˈzɔːstɪd/ *a.* 精疲力竭的
- insurance /ɪnˈʃʊrəns/ *n.* 保险
- investigator /ɪnˈvestɪɡeɪtər/ *n.* 调查员，侦查员
- patrolman /pəˈtrəʊlmən/ *n.* 巡警
- pulse /pʌls/ *n.* 脉搏
- receptionist /rɪˈsepʃənɪst/ *n.* 接待员
- siren /ˈsaɪrən/ *n.* 警报器
- sweat /swet/ *n.* 汗水 *v.* 出汗
- transportation /ˌtrænspərˈteɪʃn/ *n.* 运输，交通
- trash /træʃ/ *n.* 垃圾
- unconscious /ʌnˈkɑːnʃəs/ *a.* 不省人事的，失去知觉的
- will /wɪl/ *n.* 遗嘱

Phrases & expressions 短语和表达

- at sb.'s age 在某人的年纪

- be out of breath 喘不过气
- change over 更换，调换
- complain about ... 抱怨……
- earn a living 谋生
- emergency room 急诊室
- heart attack 心脏病发作
- make one's way toward ... 朝……方向前进
- take over 接管
- turn around 转身

Cultural notes 文化点滴

• East 43rd Street: 东 43 街。美国纽约市曼哈顿区的街道有大道（Avenue）和街（Street）两种命名方式，大道通常为南北向，街通常为东西向。

• Grand Central Station: 大中央车站，位于美国纽约市曼哈顿中城，是纽约重要的交通枢纽，也是美国最繁忙、最著名的铁路车站之一。

• in the eighties: 80 多华氏度。华氏度（°F）是温度的一种计量单位，在美国的日常生活中，多采用这种单位。华氏度 = 摄氏度 ×1.8 + 32，摄氏度 =（华氏度 – 32）÷1.8。

• police officer: 警员，一种警衔。美国纽约市警察局（NYPD）的警衔由低到高主要有 officer（警员）、detective（警探）、sergeant（警司）、lieutenant（警督）、captain（警监）等。

• Queens: 昆斯区，美国纽约市的五个行政区之一，也是其中面积最大、人口第二多的行政区。

• 911: 美国通用的报告紧急事件的电话号码。美国的消防电话、急救电话、报警电话都是911。

Reading exercise 阅读练习

Who said what?

Annie Clayton	Stella Delgado	Dr. Fischer	Nat Marley

a) "Sure you're feeling all right, Annie?"

b) "Just give me a minute. It's this pain in my chest."

c) "Someone call 911. Get an ambulance! "

d) "Nat, when are we going to get air conditioning?"

e) "So you're the guy who saved Mrs. Clayton at Grand Central?"

f) "Nat, can you find me a lawyer? I want to make a will."

Chapter 2

New words 生词

- agency /ˈeɪdʒənsi/ *n.* 事务所
- cab /kæb/ *n.* 出租车
- carpet /ˈkɑːrpɪt/ *n.* 地毯
- confused /kənˈfjuːzd/ *a.* 迷惑的，糊涂的
- elevator /ˈelɪveɪtər/ *n.* 电梯
- fashionable /ˈfæʃnəbl/ *a.* 时尚的
- laughter /ˈlæftər/ *n.* 笑声
- license /ˈlaɪsns/ *n.* 执照
- lobby /ˈlɑːbi/ *n.* 大堂，大厅
- messenger /ˈmesɪndʒər/ *n.* 送信者
- professional /prəˈfeʃənl/ *n.* 专业人士

- stare /ster/ *v.* & *n.* 凝视，注视
- uptown /ˌʌpˈtaʊn/ *ad.* 离开市中心；在（或向）市郊

Phrases & expressions 短语和表达

- at one time 曾经有一个时期，一度
- be full of ... 充满……
- call on ... 短暂访问……
- get down to ... 开始……，着手……

Cultural notes 文化点滴

- Albany: 奥尔巴尼，美国纽约州的首府，位于纽约州的中东部。
- Assam tea: 阿萨姆红茶，产于印度东北部的阿萨姆邦。它以香气浓郁、口感厚重而闻名，属于烈茶，带有淡淡的麦芽香、玫瑰香。
- Cary Grant: 加里·格兰特（1904—1986），美国著名英裔影星。1970 年，他获得第 42 届奥斯卡奖终身成就奖；1999 年，他被美国电影学会评选为“百年来最伟大的男演员”第二名。
- Central Park: 中央公园，坐落于美国纽约市曼哈顿区的中心，是世界上最大的人造自然景观之一，被称为纽约的后花园。
- Columbus Circle: 哥伦布圆环，美国纽约市曼哈顿区的一个地标，以克里斯托弗·哥伦布命名，于 1905 年建成。建成之后，哥伦布圆环车站也是纽约市的一个重要交通枢纽。
- Darjeeling tea: 大吉岭红茶，产于印度西孟加拉邦、喜马拉雅山麓的大吉岭高原。
- Great Depression: 经济大萧条，1929 年至 1933 年发源于美国的全球性经济危机。

• Joan Crawford: 琼·克劳馥（1904—1977），好莱坞黄金时代著名女影星，曾凭《欲海情魔》获得第 18 届奥斯卡奖最佳女主角奖（1946 年）。

• Syracuse: 锡拉丘兹，位于美国纽约州中部，绰号雪城、盐城，是纽约州中部地区的经济和教育中心。

Reading exercise 阅读练习

Look at the words *in italics*. Who is *me*, *we*, *I*, etc.?

Martha Bianchi	Stella Delgado
Mrs. Joanna Whittaker	Nat Marley

a) I would like your agency to do a special service for *me*.

b) *We* could be visiting several million dollars so we had to look cool and fresh.

c) "Martha does everything for me – *I* never leave the apartment."

d) *Someone* didn't like being called part of the furniture.

e) *She* knew exactly what to do. I'm no good in situations like these.

f) "You know, *you* look so much like my poor dead husband."

Chapter 3

New words 生词

• attorney /əˈtɜːrni/ *n.* 律师

• cent /sent/ *n.* 美分

• client /ˈklaɪənt/ *n.* 客户

- completely /kəmˈpliːtli/ *ad.* 完全地
- doubtfully /ˈdaʊtfəli/ *ad.* 怀疑地
- expense /ɪkˈspens/ *n.* 花销
- fee /fiː/ *n.* 酬金
- fry /fraɪ/ *v.* 油煎，油炸
- instruction /ɪnˈstrʌkʃn/ *n.* 指示
- remain /rɪˈmeɪn/ *v.* 保持
- sharply /ˈʃɑːrpli/ *ad.* 严厉地
- sherry /ˈʃeri/ *n.* 雪利酒
- sidewalk /ˈsaɪdwɔːk/ *n.* 人行道
- strength /streŋθ/ *n.* 力量
- typewriter /ˈtaɪpraɪtər/ *n.* 打字机
- upset /ʌpˈset/ *v.* 使烦恼，使生气
- witness /ˈwɪtnəs/ *n.* 证人

Phrases & expressions 短语和表达

- escape into ... 逃进……
- in memory of ... 为了纪念……
- lose count 数不清
- make a promise 承诺
- take advantage of ... 欺骗……，占……的便宜；利用……

Reading exercise 阅读练习

Match the beginnings and endings.

______ 1) Mrs. Whittaker asked Marley to find a lawyer

______ 2) Stella wondered why

______ 3) Mrs. Whittaker was surprised

______ 4) Mrs. Whittaker wanted to leave Marley everything

______ 5) Marley noticed the photo of Tom Whittaker

______ 6) Marley asked Wilma Patterson to persuade

a) but give nothing to her son and daughter.

b) so she could make a will.

c) Mrs. Whittaker to change her will.

d) and realized how similar they both looked.

e) to meet a female lawyer.

f) Mrs. Whittaker called Marley "Tom."

Chapter 4

New words 生词

- apparently /əˈpærəntli/ *ad.* 明显地
- avoid /əˈvɔɪd/ *v.* 避免
- awful /ˈɔːfl/ *a.* 糟糕的
- bartender /ˈbɑːrtendər/ *n.* 酒保
- booth /buːθ/ *n.* 小亭子
- cheerful /ˈtʃɪrfl/ *a.* 快乐的
- community /kəˈmjuːnəti/ *n.* 社区
- dawn /dɔːn/ *n.* 黎明
- diner /ˈdaɪnər/ *n.* 路边的小饭馆
- eagle /ˈiːgl/ *n.* 鹰
- height /haɪt/ *n.* 高度
- metal /ˈmetl/ *a.* 金属的
- plastic /ˈplæstɪk/ *a.* 塑料的
- skyscraper /ˈskaɪskreɪpər/ *n.* 摩天大楼
- takeout /ˈteɪkaʊt/ *n.* 外卖

- tattoo /tæˈtuː/ *n.* 文身
- track /træk/ *n.* 轨道
- underneath /ˌʌndərˈniːθ/ *prep.* & *ad.* 在（……）下面
- wander /ˈwɑːndər/ *v.* 漫步，漫游

Phrases & expressions 短语和表达

- break sb.'s heart 伤某人的心
- depend on ... 依靠……
- dream of ... 梦想……
- electric fan 电风扇
- go to pieces 支离破碎
- help out sb. 帮某人一把
- leave sb. alone 不打扰某人
- no point (in) doing sth. 做某事没有意义
- raise sb.'s hope 燃起某人的希望

Cultural notes 文化点滴

• five feet ten inches: 五英尺十英寸，相当于 177.8 厘米。1 英尺等于 12 英寸，1 英寸等于 2.54 厘米。

• housing project: 国民住宅，主要指由政府计划，用以出售、出租、贷款自建或提供贷款利息补贴，供较低收入家庭居住的住宅。

• Macy's: 梅西百货公司，美国著名的连锁百货公司，主要经营高档品牌的服装、鞋帽、化妆品等。

• Pan Am: 泛美世界航空（Pan American World Airways），自 20 世纪 30 年代至 1991 年倒闭，一直是美国的主要航空公司。

• Riker's Island jail: 赖克斯岛监狱，位于美国纽约市，纽约人通常称

其为“那座岛”，这里有全美最危险的罪犯和最严厉的狱警。赖克斯岛监狱是不少电影和小说虚构人物坐牢的地方。

- Sam Adams: 萨姆·亚当斯啤酒，产于美国，曾多次获得“全美国最棒的啤酒”称号和美国“大啤酒节金奖”。
- You ain't seen nothing yet: 你还什么都没看到呢。这里的 ain't 相当于 have not（根据语境，ain't 相当于 am not、is not、are not、has not 或 have not)，多在非正式口语中使用。

Reading exercise 阅读练习

Put the events in the right order.

a) Marley was surprised to see electric fans in the office.
b) Leona took Marley uptown to Annie's underground home.
c) Annie told Marley about her lost son, Jackie.
d) Annie asked Marley to find Jackie before she died.
e) Marley took the box to Annie in Bellevue Hospital.
f) Ed Winchester told Marley about Tom Whittaker's airline business.

Chapter 5

New words 生词

- blonde /blɑːnd/ *n.* 金发女郎
- buddy /ˈbʌdi/ *n.*（称呼不认识的男子）老兄；朋友
- disagreement /ˌdɪsəˈgriːmənt/ *n.* 分歧
- extra /ˈekstrə/ *a.* 额外的

- marriage /ˈmærɪdʒ/ *n.* 婚姻
- passenger /ˈpæsɪndʒər/ *n.* 乘客
- photocopy /ˈfəʊtəʊkɑːpi/ *n.* 复印件
- pilot /ˈpaɪlət/ *n.* 飞行员

Cultural note 文化点滴

- Marilyn Monroe: 玛丽莲·梦露（1926—1962），美国著名女演员。1999 年，她被美国电影学会评选为“百年来最伟大的女演员”第六名。梦露是影迷心中永远的性感女神和流行文化的代表性人物。

Reading exercise 阅读练习

True or false?

a) Tom Whittaker had been a pilot in the First World War.
b) Tom Whittaker had started an airline business in the 1950s.
c) Tom Whittaker had been a good husband.
d) Mrs. Whittaker sometimes left the apartment.
e) Mrs. Whittaker's son and daughter used to visit her.
f) Martha was the only person who Mrs. Whittaker saw now.

Chapter 6

New words 生词

- buck /bʌk/ *n.* 美元
- cop /kɑːp/ *n.* 警察
- customer /ˈkʌstəmər/ *n.* 顾客
- description /dɪˈskrɪpʃn/ *n.* 描述

- headquarters /ˈhedkwɔːrtərz/ *n.* 总部
- intend /ɪnˈtend/ *v.* 打算
- poisonous /ˈpɔɪzənəs/ *a.* 恶毒的
- tough /tʌf/ *a.* 粗暴的，凶恶的

Phrases & expressions 短语和表达

- be in trouble 陷入麻烦
- break down 崩溃，出故障
- clean up ... 把……打扫干净
- move sb. on（尤指警察）命令某人离开某地
- reach for ... 伸手去够……
- set up sth. 安排某事，策划某事
- stick sb.'s nose in ... 插手……
- turn up 找到，发现；出现，露面

Cultural notes 文化点滴

- Alphabet City: 字母城，位于美国纽约市东村，因为这里的大道以A、B、C、D 依次命名而得名。
- Big Apple: 大苹果，美国纽约市的别称。
- cross one's fingers: 把同一只手的中指叠在食指上，两指交叉（crossed）成 X 状，像十字架的形状。这个手势代表“好运，祝福”的意思。

Reading exercise 阅读练习

Who gave Marley the information?

bartender at Vazac's	Joe Blaney	Wilma Patterson
Mr. Wiseman	Lieutenant Brandstein	

a) Jackie Clayton was not in prison.
b) Jackie's business was buying what people had stolen.
c) Jackie could be working for Wiseman Cabs.
d) Jackie's old boss wanted to find him.
e) Mrs. Whittaker's opinion of Marley.
f) Charlie Whittaker's home phone number.
g) Charlie Whittaker had agreed to set up a family meeting.

Chapter 7

New words 生词

- develop /dɪˈveləp/ *v.* 冲洗（照片）
- explode /ɪkˈspləʊd/ *v.* 大发雷霆，勃然大怒
- film /fɪlm/ *n.* 胶卷
- mood /muːd/ *n.* 情绪
- promising /ˈprɑːmɪsɪŋ/ *a.* 有希望的
- property /ˈprɑːpərti/ *n.* 财产
- sauna /ˈsaʊnə/ *n.* 桑拿
- suitcase /ˈsuːtkeɪs/ *n.* 手提箱

Phrases & expressions 短语和表达

- as long as 只要

- be found not guilty of ... 被判无……罪
- get sb.'s hands on ... 找到……，得到……
- hold on 坚持
- keep away from ... 远离……
- lock up 锁好门窗
- only just 才，刚刚
- talk sth. over 详细讨论某事
- up to ... 正在做……（秘密或不该做的事）

Reading exercise 阅读练习

Complete the summary with the names of the characters.

Dr. Fischer	Captain Oldenberg	Annie Clayton
Jackie Clayton	Stella Delgado	Ed Winchester
Mr. Wiseman/Ernst Weissmann	Joe Blaney	

_________ had been taking photos of Wiseman Cabs all afternoon. _________ phoned from the hospital to say that _________ was getting much worse. At McFadden's Bar, _________ showed Marley a newspaper story. Five years ago, _________ and _________ had been found not guilty of buying stolen property. Marley compared the newspaper photo with Joe's photo, realized that _________ and _________ were the same person and called _________ at police headquarters. Finally, _________ persuaded Marley to buy air conditioning for the office.

Chapter 8

New words 生词

- certificate /sərˈtɪfɪkət/ *n.* 证明书

- chip /tʃɪp/ *n.* 碎片，碎渣；筹码（用于赌博）
- establish /ɪˈstæblɪʃ/ *v.* 确定，证实
- funeral /ˈfjuːnərəl/ *n.* 葬礼

Phrases & expressions 短语和表达

- be supposed to do/be sth. 应该做 / 是某事
- for sb.'s liking 适合某人的口味（或愿望）
- get rid of ... 摆脱……
- take sb.'s word for it 相信某人的话

Reading exercises 阅读练习

1. Match the questions to the answers.

_____ 1) "Has the doctor already seen her?"

_____ 2) "When did you last see Mrs. Whittaker alive?"

_____ 3) "Do you normally give Mrs. Whittaker her pills?"

_____ 4) "You haven't touched anything in her room?"

_____ 5) "Did Mrs. Whittaker take sleeping pills regularly, Doctor?"

_____ 6) "Now, Mr. Marley, surely you don't think ...?"

a) "No sir ... I know that from detective stories."

b) "Sure I do. Two at bedtime to help her sleep."

c) "Yes. I suggested she take them."

d) "Why should he? Not much he can do for her now."

e) "I don't know what to think, Doctor. That's the problem."

f) "When I took in her hot chocolate ... Ten o'clock last night."

2. Did Mrs. Whittaker die naturally or was she murdered? What do you think?

Chapter 9

New words 生词

- cell /sel/ *n.* 牢房
- commission /kəˈmɪʃn/ *n.* 委员会
- limousine /ˈlɪməziːn/ *n.* 轿车，豪华大轿车
- meatpacking /ˈmiːtˌpækɪŋ/ *n.* 肉类加工
- thoughtfully /ˈθɔːtfəli/ *ad.* 若有所思地

Phrases & expressions 短语和表达

- at arm's length 一臂之距
- be caught up in ... 被困在……中
- catch up with ... 抓住……
- frighten the life out of sb. 把某人吓得要死

Reading exercise 阅读练习

Match the descriptions to the characters.

Martha Bianchi	Joe Blaney	Jackie Clayton
Nat Marley	Mr. Wiseman	

a) "You could be my father's ghost."

b) "Her behavior's very strange."

c) Physically, he seemed to be in worse shape than Mrs. Whittaker.

d) Sitting in his car with his hat pulled down over his eyes, he looked just like a guy sleeping.

e) He just looked like any normal guy going about his normal business.

f) I was tired, hot, and hungry.

Chapter 10

New words 生词

- autopsy /ˈɔːtɑːpsi/ *n.* 尸检，验尸
- checkbook /ˈtʃekbʊk/ *n.* 支票簿
- definitely /ˈdefɪnətli/ *ad.* 绝对地
- ketchup /ˈketʃəp/ *n.* 调味番茄酱
- lipstick /ˈlɪpstɪk/ *n.* 口红，唇膏
- package /ˈpækɪdʒ/ *n.* 包裹
- tub /tʌb/ *n.* 盆

Phrases & expressions 短语和表达

- calm down 冷静下来
- check into a hotel 入住酒店
- in a mess 一团糟
- leave sth. with ... 把某物留给……
- look from side to side 左右张望
- make up sth. 准备某物
- owe sb. an apology 欠某人一句道歉
- stand in sb.'s way 挡着某人的路
- stick to ... 粘在……

Cultural note 文化点滴

- Chase Manhattan: 大通曼哈顿银行，美国金融业巨头之一，大型商业银行，总部设于纽约。2000 年，大通曼哈顿银行和摩根银行合

并成为摩根大通银行（JPMorgan Chase）。

Reading exercise 阅读练习

Are the following sentences fact or possibility? Write "F" or "P."

a) Nobody knew where Martha was.

b) Martha had murdered Mrs. Whittaker.

c) Martha enjoyed reading detective stories.

d) Martha had taken all Mrs. Whittaker's money.

e) At first, Jackie didn't believe Marley.

f) Jackie was going to see his mother before she died.

Chapter 11

New words 生词

- booklet /ˈbʊklət/ *n.* 小册子
- casino /kəˈsiːnəʊ/ *n.* 赌场
- gambling /ˈɡæmblɪŋ/ *n.* 赌博
- overdraw /ˌəʊvərˈdrɔː/ *v.*（银行账户）透支
- still /stɪl/ *a.* 静止的，不动的

Phrases & expressions 短语和表达

- look over one's shoulder for ... 小心提防……
- look through ... 浏览……
- more or less 大约，差不多
- pull sth. down 拆毁（建筑物）
- rather than 而不是

Cultural notes 文化点滴

• Atlantic City: 大西洋城，美国新泽西州城市，世界四大赌城之一，美国第二大赌城。

• Las Vegas: 拉斯维加斯，美国内华达州最大的城市。拉斯维加斯位居世界四大赌城之首，是一座以赌博业为中心的旅游、购物、度假城市，拥有"世界娱乐之都"和"结婚之都"的美称。

Reading exercise 阅读练习

Correct the mistakes in the summary.

Jackie had been hiding from Wiseman for the last six months because he wanted an exciting life. Martha had taken out thousands of dollars from Mrs. Whittaker's bank account. Marley noticed that Martha had underlined sentences in a book called *The Perfect Crime*; Joe thought Martha's message "Gone to play ball" probably meant that she was interested in baseball. Marley and Joe went to look for Martha in Las Vegas, which was seven hours away from New York.

Chapter 12

New words 生词

- affect /əˈfekt/ *v.* 影响
- expressway /ɪkˈspresweɪ/ *n.* 快速干道，高速公路
- irregular /ɪˈregjələr/ *a.* 不规则的
- scream /skriːm/ *v.* 尖叫

- tiny /ˈtaɪni/ *a.* 微小的

Phrases & expressions 短语和表达

- by choice 出于自己的选择
- wake sb. up 叫醒某人

Cultural note 文化点滴

- roulette: 轮盘，一种赌场常见的博彩游戏。

Reading exercise 阅读练习

Who did what?

Martha Bianchi	Joe Blaney	Annie Clayton
Jackie Clayton	Dr. Fischer	Nat Marley

a) Who never left his mother's bedside?

b) Who found Martha in the Golden Palace?

c) Who won on number 7?

d) Who admitted to the murder of Mrs. Whittaker?

e) Who told Jackie that his mother was dead?

f) Who had never given up hope for Jackie?

g) Who had tears in his eyes?

Chapter 13

New words 生词

- bang /bæŋ/ *n.* 猛撞，巨响
- crash /kræʃ/ *n.* 碎裂声；碰撞
- increasingly /ɪnˈkriːsɪŋli/ *ad.* 越来越多地，不断增加地
- midtown /ˈmɪdtaʊn/ *n.* 市中心区

Phrases & expressions 短语和表达

- as for ... 至于……
- be tried for ... 因……而受到审判
- in return 作为回报
- in the first place 最初
- light up sth. 点亮某物
- no picnic 不是件轻松愉快的事

Cultural note 文化点滴

• Coney Island: 科尼艾兰，美国纽约市布鲁克林区的半岛。科尼艾兰是美国最早的大型游乐城，星际太空乐园是该地的主要游览项目之一，深受孩子们喜爱。

Reading exercises 阅读练习

1. Tick (√) the things which were in Annie Clayton's box.

   a) Annie's will

   b) letter from Annie to Jackie

c) letter from Tom Whittaker to Annie

d) letter from Tom Whittaker to Jackie

e) family photographs

f) pile of money

g) stock certificates

2. What is the relationship between ...

a) Tom Whittaker and Jackie Clayton?

b) Charlie Whittaker and Betty Osborne?

c) Jackie Clayton and Charlie Whittaker?

Chapter 14

New words 生词

- local /ˈləʊkl/ *a.* 当地的
- politician /ˌpɑːləˈtɪʃn/ *n.* 政治家

Phrases & expressions 短语和表达

- provide for ... 供养……，抚养……
- set foot in ... 访问……，参观……

Reading exercise 阅读练习

Which characters ...

Jackie Clayton	Betty Osborne
Charlie Whittaker	all of them

a) lost their mothers?

b) refused love to a mother?

c) have a lot in common?

d) came from the Bronx?

e) had a difficult childhood?

f) got into trouble on the streets?

g) had a cold, unloving father?

h) did something to improve people's lives?

Translation
参考译文

贫富之间

第 1 章　城市的夏天

第5页

他们说如果不喜欢酷热，就离开厨房。如果不喜欢酷热，七月中旬就离开纽约。度假的人都在山里或是长岛上，在任何比这个城市更凉爽的地方。而我，我有工作要做，有钱要挣。当我离开在昆斯区的公寓楼时，热浪袭来。气温已经高达 80 多华氏度，才早上七点，我就出汗了。这又将是一个酷热难耐的日子，该搭乘 7 号线列车去曼哈顿了。

我叫马利，纳特·马利。我对纽约这座城市了如指掌，纽约是我的一部分，融在我的血液里。我曾在纽约市警察局任职十五年，在这期间，我见到了这座城市最优越和最不堪的生活。离开纽约市警察局之后，我成了一名私家侦探。尽管挣不了那么多钱，但我自己当老板，不用听命于他人，我更喜欢这样。

第6页

在大中央车站，成群的上班族快速出站走向第 42 街。车站里通常会有一些无家可归的人，想趁着警察还没驱赶他们先赚上几美元。如果你每天都走同样的路，便会熟悉人们的脸。但是今天，我没有看见一个流浪者，也许他们正在第42街晒太阳。

突然一个声音呼唤道：“嘿，纳特，你认不出我了吗？”

我转过身。一位穿着昂贵大衣和裙子的老妇人站在那里，是安妮，一个真正的纽约人，一个我在纽约市警察局当巡警时就认识的流浪人员之一。

“你喜欢我的大衣吗，纳特？我在垃圾堆里找到的。”

“七月穿冬衣？你一定热坏了吧。我喜欢这件大衣，但是你看起来气色不太好，安妮。”

“我还好，纳特。不管怎样，冬衣值钱，所以不管晴天还是雪天它都得跟我待在一起。”

我仔细地打量她，她跟平时不太一样。我说不出具体是什么，但是她变了。

“你确定没事吗，安妮？”

“我吗，纳特？从来没感觉这么好过。”

第7页

也许她只是因为在她这个年纪还要在街上谋生计而疲惫不堪罢了，但是直觉告诉我，我应该待在她身边。

“我给你买早饭吧，咖啡和甜甜圈？”我提议道。

安妮挽住我的胳膊，我们朝正门走去。突然她拽了一下我的上衣。

“嘿，别走这么快，纳特。等我一分钟，我胸部这里疼。”

我仔细地观察她，她脸上汗如雨下。我们并没有走多远，但是她已经上气不接下气。她紧紧地握住我的手，她的皮肤摸起来冰凉。

“我的天！”她喊道。

她伸手去抓胸口，眼睛和嘴巴因为疼痛张得大大的。然后她倒在我的脚下，失去了意识。这是心脏病发作。我摸摸她的手腕，没有脉搏。她的胸部也没有起伏，她没有呼吸了。我没有时间思考，我回想起在纽约市警察局接受的所有培训。先人工呼吸，让头向后仰，捏住鼻子，打开嘴巴，检查气道。用我的嘴唇封住她的嘴，呼气，停，再呼气。然后我把双手放在她的胸部按压，重复十五次。我抬头看了看围在我们周围的人。

第9页

“谁打一下 911 吧，叫辆救护车！这里谁受过急救训练?”我问道。

一个男人紧张地走上前来。“我刚上过急救课。”他说。

“开始人工呼吸，然后我们互换。”

我们抢救了整整五分钟。我又摸了一下安妮的手腕，这回有脉搏了。接着她胸部开始有起伏。最后，我听到了救护车的笛声。

救护人员接手，把安妮送到了在第 42 街等待的救护车上。我知道像她这种人是不会有医疗保险的。

“你们要把她送到贝尔维尤医院?”我问道。

“是的。”

“这是我的名片。任何关于医院账单的问题，让他们打电话给我。”

我究竟该怎么支付医院账单则是另一回事。

一名警官过来向我了解情况。他刚走开，一名来自《每日新闻》的记者就向我跑来。

“我能问你几个问题吗，先生？这会是一篇很棒的新闻报道。”

我不介意，这件事也许对生意有好处。

第10页

从大中央车站到我在东 43 街 220 号的办公室，步行需要五分钟。楼里的大多数办公室都有自己的空调，我的没有，所以又热又不舒服。

我到的时候办公室很安静，没有任何惊喜。七月份生意通常很冷清，连坏人也去度假了。

我的私人助理斯特拉·德尔加多已经在她的工位上了。她看起来不仅疲惫，还气呼呼的。

“纳特，我们什么时候能装空调？”她问道，“根本没法儿工作，看看你衬衫上的汗！”

“我刚才在大中央车站跪在地上，”我说，“救了一个老太太的命。在这么热的天可不容易。”

我告诉斯特拉发生了什么，她不再抱怨屋里热了。

“我们去看看她怎么样了吧。”她提议道。

纽约的私家侦探一般不使用公共交通工具，但我不一样。我和斯特拉在第二大道乘坐 15 路公交车前往市中心，然后向东步行一个街区，到达坐落在第一大道的医院。我向接待员介绍自己。

“我叫纳特·马利，是安妮·克莱顿的好朋友。她刚刚被收治到急诊室。我们必须得见见她，小姐。你看……”

第11页

“抱歉，只有家属才能进急诊室。”接待员说。

“你看，小姐。她比我妻子更像我的家人。”我说。

这是实话，离婚以后我就没怎么见过马利夫人。

“我给急诊室打个电话，看看他们怎么说。”接待员回复道。

我们得到允许去探视。一名医生正在给安妮检查心脏，我和斯特拉在检查室外面等待。最后医生终于出来了，并介绍了她自己。

“马利先生？我是费希尔医生。按照规定只有家属才可以来这里，但这是个特例。所以你就是在大中央车站救了克莱顿夫人的那个人？你干得漂亮。”

“她会好起来吗，医生？”我问道。

她的脸向我透露了我需要知道的一切。“她是位斗士，但是她有非常严重的心脏病。”她说。

安妮正在睡觉，我们等了一个多小时才被允许进入房间探视。她看起来疲惫不堪，但是见到我还是笑了。

第12页

“纳特，见到你太好了。”她说，“还有，谢谢。”

“这不算什么，安妮。我每天都挽救生命。”我说。

“纳特，我一直在想，我可能没剩多少时日了。今天早上的事并不稀奇，我多年来一直有心脏病。纳特，你能帮我找位律师吗？我想立份遗嘱。”

我想知道安妮死后要给谁留些什么东西。但不管怎么说，我同意了她的要求。我认识一位出色的家庭律师，威尔玛·帕特森。我打电话给她，她答应下午来医院。

这就是这个离奇故事的开始，故事中的两位老妇人来自纽约社会的两极——上流社会和底层社会。两位老妇人不曾谋面，生活也截然不同。这是一个关于她们的人生如何交织在一起的故事。

第 2 章　中央公园西大道

第13页

第二天早上，我的照片便同整个故事一起出现在了《每日新闻》的内页上，标题是《生命垂危的女士得救》。故事的开头写道：

“昨日，若不是私家侦探纳特·马利反应迅速，无家可归的纽约人安妮·克莱顿已命丧大中央车站。”

大约十一点钟，送信员送来一封信。地址是工整地手写的。我有了一个新的职位：

“致纳特·马利先生，马利调查事务所高级侦探。”

“哇，这使你显得很重要，纳特！”斯特拉说。

这封信来自乔安娜·惠特克女士，信上的地址是中央公园西大道 25 号世纪公寓 1543 号。那是个富人区。世纪公寓是 20 世纪 30 年代经济大萧条之前建成的最后一批时尚公寓住宅楼。

第14页

信中这样写道：

亲爱的马利先生：

我刚刚在《每日新闻》上读到你的故事。我希望你的事务所可以帮我一个特殊的忙。我需要一位专业人士。

我不离开我的公寓，希望可以私下和你谈谈。看门人会迎接你。你可以在任何一天的下午 12:00 到 1:00 来找我。

你真诚的

乔安娜·惠特克（夫人）

“你怎么看，斯特拉？”我问道。

“有意思。”斯特拉说。

“我们要去拜访这位女士吗？我们可以现在就去——这里没有什么事。”

只有这一次，我看起来很精神。我穿上了一件干净的衬衫，还有刚从干洗店取回来的高级夹克。斯特拉也穿上了她的新套装。我们看起来完全是专业人士。

“斯特拉，我们搭出租车吧。”我说。

“出租车！你真的没事吧？”她惊讶地问道。

我从没有感觉这么好过。我们可能要拜访有几百万美元的大客户，因此我们得看上去既酷又清爽。通常，我讨厌花钱搭出租车，但是如果你想在七月份看起来体面，就不能走路。

第15页

那时是十一点半，车辆的速度并不比走路快多少。我为这些出租车司机感到难过。我们的车缓慢穿过市区，抵达哥伦布圆环，然后沿着中央公园西大道行驶到世纪公寓住宅区。这是曼哈顿最好的地段之一。

我们到那里时，我向看门人报了名字。

“惠特克夫人正在等你，马利先生。但是我得先通报她一声，以免这位老妇人太激动。”

他拿起电话，等了一分多钟没有任何回应。

“这可能得花些时间。”看门人解释道。

“她有时会有些糊涂。喂，是玛莎吗？我是大厅的鲍勃。我这里有几位惠特克夫人的访客……是的，内森·马利先生和他的私人助理斯特拉·德尔加多女士……是的，我这就让他们上去。”

电梯里全部由深色原木装饰，铺着厚厚的地毯，挂着几面镜子。如果这只是电梯，想象一下公寓会是什么样子。我这辈子会有机会住在这种地方吗？以我的收入水平，只能在梦里了。我按了公寓的门铃后等待着。一分钟后，我再次按了门铃，门终于开了，一位身材高大的中年女子不悦地瞪着我。

第16页

“你是马利先生？”她问道。

“是的，女士。还有我的助理斯特拉·德尔加多女士。”

“出示一下你的执照。”

我递给她我的私家侦探执照。

“等一会儿。”她说完便在我面前关上了门。

又是一阵等待。她返回来，一言不发地带我们走进客厅，一位老妇人正在客厅里等待。

“马利先生和德尔加多小姐，你们好。我是乔安娜·惠特克。请坐。玛莎，给客人们上茶。”

我环顾房间，里面到处都是20世纪40年代的精美家具。多年来什么都没有改变，我感觉自己仿佛置身于好莱坞的一部老电影中。我在想接下来谁会走进来——加里·格兰特还是琼·克劳馥？

玛莎端着杯子和两个茶壶回到客厅。她看起来并不太乐意接待访客。她粗壮的手臂端起重重的茶具显得不费吹灰之力。

“阿萨姆红茶还是大吉岭红茶，马利先生？”惠特克夫人问道。

第17页

我并不知道它们的区别，但是我不会承认这一点。

“阿萨姆红茶，谢谢你，夫人。加三块糖。”

“啊，太好了！我喜欢爱吃甜食的男人。就像我那可怜的丈夫以前那样。你呢，德尔加多小姐？”

“大吉岭红茶，谢谢。”斯特拉回答道。

第18页

“我们结婚的时候，我丈夫买下了这个地方。”惠特克夫人说，“从那时起我就住在这里。这间公寓曾经充满了欢笑和幸福。但是自从我可怜的丈夫去世以后，就只剩下我自己和玛莎了。玛莎为我打理一切——我从不离开公寓。她在这个家很多年了，几乎是家具的一部分。”

厨房有打碎玻璃的声音，惠特克夫人没有听到。有人并不喜欢被称为家具的一部分。

“你有什么家人吗？”斯特拉问道。

“一个儿子和一个女儿。他们不住在本市。查利在奥尔巴尼，贝蒂在锡拉丘兹。我希望能多见见他们，特别是孙辈，但是……”

这位老妇人的眼里噙满了泪水。斯特拉握着她的手，她很清楚该怎么做。我不擅长应对这种场合。

“好了，别哭了，夫人。我们理解。”斯特拉说。

“你们理解？……我很抱歉，小姐。”

“不用道歉。”我说。

“谢谢你们，我没事了。”她说。然后她看着我。“现在，汤姆，”她说，“我们开始谈正事吧。”

“汤姆？”我眼睛盯着她问道。

第19页

“我说汤姆了吗？”她问道，“哦，我真傻！我的错。你知道，你和我那可怜的死去的丈夫长得太像了。我刚才说到哪儿了？哦，对，马利先生，我需要一名律师。”

第3章　遗嘱

第20页

“惠特克夫人，”我说，“我不是律师。”

“我也许老了，但我还没有完全傻掉。”老妇人回答道，“我希望你帮我找到一名律师。”

“电话簿在哪里？”我问道，“我会告诉你该给谁打电话。”

“你没明白。我想让你找一名优秀的律师，并且把他带到这里来。找一个我可以相信的人，这和我的遗嘱有关。”

惠特克夫人打开手提包，拿出一沓百元钞票。我很多年没有在一个地方见过这么多钱了。

“你怎么收费，马利先生？”

“一千美元一天外加其他开销。但不是现在，夫人，是我完成工作的时候。我不会带着这么多钱到处走动，这可能会有危险。”

我们离开凉爽的世纪公寓大厅，步行到中央公园西大道。如果你不喜欢炎热的天气，那就找个酒吧。我们就是这么做的。穿过公园步行一小段路到达绿苑酒吧。我不会选择来这种地方喝酒，酒水又贵，游客又多。但是这里近，当天气热到足以在马路上煎鸡蛋的时候，离得近很重要。

第21页

我们坐在一个安静的角落，点了两杯冰镇啤酒，谈论着我们刚刚见到的两位女士。

“多么奇怪的生活方式！”斯特拉说。

“是啊。你能想象吗？足不出户。”我回应道，“在我看来，玛莎为惠特克夫人打理所有的事情。她看起来仿佛力大无穷，不过是个奇怪的女人罢了。我可不想在黑暗冷清的街上碰到她。”

斯特拉一言不发，我看得出她在思考。

“惠特克夫人也非常奇怪。”她最终说道，“她有家人，那她为什么没有自己的家庭律师呢？还有我看不到她孩子的任何照片。只有结婚照片和她丈夫的照片。然后她还叫你‘汤姆’，她认为你是谁呢？

她死而复生的丈夫?”

“谁知道究竟是怎么回事!”我说,“但是担心这个不会帮我们挣到钱。我们走吧,去找那位律师。”

我和斯特拉回到办公室,我给威尔玛·帕特森打了一个电话。三点前我们做好了安排。我们回到世纪公寓搭乘电梯上到15层和威尔玛会面。玛莎一言不发地领我们进屋。

第22页

“啊,马利先生和德尔加多小姐。但是我的律师在哪儿呢?”惠特克夫人问道。

威尔玛打断她。“惠特克夫人,我是威尔玛·帕特森,帕特森和斯科菲尔德律师所的高级合伙人”

“我不相信你!”惠特克夫人严厉地说。

“惠特克夫人,”我说,“帕特森夫人是我认识的最好的律师。相信我。”

惠特克夫人满腹狐疑地看着我,我只是点了点头,笑了笑。终于她放松下来。

“好吧,好吧。现如今这时代,我没想到会是一位女律师。现在请坐下吧。你们会和我一起喝一杯雪利酒的,是不是?玛莎!”

玛莎拿着瓶子和杯子走进来,她看起来气呼呼的。惠特克夫人挥手让她去厨房,甚至连声“谢谢”都没有说。

“你要甜的还是无糖的,马利先生?”她问道。

我不喝雪利酒,但是我不想让惠特克夫人失望,要了甜的。

“非常好的选择,汤姆。”她微笑着说,“哦,天哪!我又叫你汤姆。因为汤姆总是喜欢甜的雪利酒,你也是。现在马利先生,如果你愿意请和德尔加多小姐在这里等一下。我要和帕特森夫人在书房谈事情。”

第23页

我知道这需要时间。我让自己舒舒服服的，又多喝了几杯雪利酒。过了一会儿，斯特拉睡着了。我开始算客厅里家具的价钱，在计算到五万美元的时候算不过来了。

一小时后，威尔玛回来了，她看起来很焦虑。“纳特，我们有个问题，”她说，“惠特克夫人想让你变富有。”

“这是个问题吗？”我问道。

“她的儿子和女儿不会得到一分钱的情况下就是个问题。我已经跟她谈论过这个问题，但是她不听，她想把所有的遗产都给你。她在报纸上读到你的故事，说你让她想起了她死去的丈夫，汤姆。还说除你之外她想不出更好的人来托付所有的财产。”

厨房的门开着，突然间有更多玻璃破碎的声音。是玛莎那里发生了很多意外，还是她正在听着我们说的每个字，而她并不喜欢所听到的内容？

“那现在怎么样了？”我问道。

“最终，我没有太多的选择。”威尔玛说，“一名律师只能服从客户的指示。”

第24页

“我不喜欢这样，”我说，“你必须得跟她的家人沟通一下，并安排一次会面。否则我将会陷入一场家庭战争之中。”

“同意。”她回答道，“但是我不敢保证什么。”

威尔玛回到书房。然后我听到有人用一台古老的打字机打字的声音。又喝了几杯雪利酒之后，我开始头疼。我站起身来更仔细地端详汤姆·惠特克的一张照片。他大约四十几岁，身材有些发福，还脱发。真不幸，就像我一样。打字的声音持续着。五点钟，威尔玛走出来让斯特拉作为证人在遗嘱上签字，看门人被从楼下叫上来做第二证人。几分钟之后，大家都回到客厅。惠特克夫人看起来很满意。

“谢谢你们大家。”惠特克夫人说，“马利先生，你的酬劳。”

她给了我一个鼓鼓囊囊的信封。

“帕特森夫人已经给我她的账单了。”惠特克夫人把另一个鼓鼓囊囊的信封给了威尔玛。

“现在，在你们走之前，每个人一份礼物。玛莎……玛莎！”

第25页

玛莎有力的手臂捧着一摞大开本的书走进房间。

“纪念我亲爱的丈夫。”惠特克夫人说。

我看了看书名——《惠特克航空历史》，汤姆·惠特克总裁著。那么这就是这个家族财产的来源。

“非常感谢你，夫人。我会好好读这本书的。”我撒谎道。

惠特克夫人给了我一个甜甜的、大大的微笑，仿佛沉浸在恋爱之中，这吓到了我。她牵起我的手。她的手全是骨头，皮肤像纸一样薄。那个时刻，我只想逃离那间公寓，永远不再回去。

“我死后你会喜欢生活在这里的，汤姆。”她说。

玛莎站在大家身后，她用恶毒的眼神瞪了惠特克夫人很久。

最终，我们逃到午后的酷热中。我在外边打开了信封，里面有两千美元，全是百元钞票。对于一天的工作而言酬劳还不错。

威尔玛·帕特森看起来有些担忧。

“纳特，一旦她的家人发现遗嘱的事情，麻烦就来了。”她说。

第26页

“我难道不知道吗！”我回答道，“你得找到她的家人，跟他们聊聊，让她更改遗嘱。”

“正如我之前所说的，我尽力而为。”威尔玛回答道。

“谢谢，”我说，“我不想让任何人觉得我占了糊涂老太太的便宜。”

第 4 章　城市街道之下

第27页

我们回到东 43 街的时候，已经六点多了，试图做任何工作都是徒劳的。我溜达到第二大道上的麦克法登酒吧。《每日新闻》的记者通常会聚集在那里，做他们最擅长的事——喝酒。

我需要信息，而且我恰巧认识那个能够帮助我的家伙——埃德·温切斯特。他曾是《每日新闻》的罪案记者，现在也还做些兼职工作。一日为记者，终身为记者。

“纳特，我的老朋友！”埃德见到我时说，“你来得正是时候。”

“是说你的酒杯空了吗，埃德？”我问道，然后向酒保挥手，“杰克！给我来萨姆·亚当斯啤酒，给埃德来杯酒。”

是时候由埃德凭自己的本事赚酒水了。我告诉他我们和惠特克夫人奇怪的会面以及遗嘱的事情，问他对这家人了解多少。我知道我可以信赖埃德——他的记忆力非常好。

第28页

埃德喝了一口酒然后说道：“嗯……汤姆·惠特克。好，他是 20 世纪 20 年代纽约和洛杉矶之间定期航空服务的创始人。这个生意在 20 世纪 50—60 年代非常成功，之后他出售了公司。我记得它成了泛美航空公司的一部分。我会看看还能发现些什么。”

“所以他们家族赚到了钱？”我问道。

“很多钱。”埃德说。

这一天过得很漫长，而且我还开始头疼。我离开酒吧，搭乘 7 号线地铁回到我在昆斯区的家。在街区那头的小饭馆买的外卖我吃不下多少。那天晚上，我躺了好几个小时都睡不着。等我终于睡着的时候，天都快亮了。早上，我没什么精神。我机械地出门去上班，脑子里没有一点儿想法或点子。接受我的建议——七月不要去纽约。

我到办公室时，斯特拉已经在工作了。办公室里并不像往常那样闷热。我能透过我办公室的门看到，她的桌子上有两台电风扇，又两台风扇。

“早上好，斯特拉。这些风扇是从哪儿来的？”我问道。

“梅西百货。”她答道，“我昨天打了电话，这是店里的最后几台了。很幸运我们能买到，这是账单。”

第29页

“这是什么？”我问道，“两百美元！你觉得我是钱造的吗？”

“没有风扇我没办法工作。”斯特拉说，“要是我不能工作，就没法儿为你赚钱。就这么简单。”

我正要争辩时电话响了，是贝尔维尤医院的费希尔医生。安妮说她要见我。很明显，是重要的事。

我到安妮的病房时，她正在床上坐着，但是她看起来很糟糕。有一位访客陪着她。

“纳特，见到你太好了。”安妮虚弱地说，“这是利昂娜，一位老朋友。利昂娜，见见纳特。他将帮助我处理一些家里的事。你不用问，纳特，无论如何我会付给你报酬的。”

“我从没想过要钱，安妮。”我说。我在那里为的是帮老朋友一把。安妮已经病得很厉害，她不知道我一天的费用是多少。

“如果干活儿不要钱，人就没办法养家糊口。”安妮说，“纳特，我希望你和利昂娜一起走。她会带你去一个你以前从未去过的地方。”

第30页

在纽约市警察局任职的十五年间，我去过纽约市大多数地方。我在想利昂娜会带我去哪里。我们离开医院向西走了四个街区，到达第28街的地铁站。然后我们乘坐上行6号线前往第103街和列克星敦大道。有些纽约人从不在东区超过第96街再往北去。对他们而言，北边的任何地方都像外国一样。在第103街，确实感觉像是另一个世界。那里没有奢华的商店、高档餐馆，或是摩天大楼。仅有的高层建筑是国民住宅——为劳动人民建造的低成本公寓。街上的人大部分是非裔和拉丁裔美国人。

“那么，有什么新鲜事吗，利昂娜？”我问道，“我过去当巡警的时候总是走这些街道。”

“耐心点儿，纳特。”她回答道，“你还什么都没看到呢。”

利昂娜带我穿过列克星敦大道，来到一幢老楼。它看起来是空的。但利昂娜一敲门，门就开了。一个身材魁梧的男人迎接利昂娜，但是随即冷冷地盯着我，指着我问道：“这个家伙来这儿做什么？”

“他没什么，”利昂娜解释道，“他很好。纳特在为安妮办点儿小事。”

第31页

利昂娜带我下了几级台阶，在底部，墙上有一个洞，她带我穿过了洞。这里伸手不见五指。

“我们这是在哪儿，利昂娜？”我问道。

“在街道下方，这是一个你不知道的城市。现在小心点儿，有辆列车正开过来。”

一列开往市区的5号线列车经过。列车窗户透出的灯光让我看清楚了我们所在的位置——地铁。有四条列车轨道，两条通往城市外围住宅区，两条通往市区，轨道旁还有一条狭窄的小路。在我们前面是一个地铁站，但是没有灯。

“欢迎来到我们的家，纳特。”利昂娜说，“这个车站废弃了，所以我们搬了进来。”

我听说过有人住在纽约地下，但是我从来没有亲眼看到过。我能看到前方有灯光。这个所谓的“家”是我童年记忆里的那种旧木质换乘亭。一位女士正坐在门边的一把扶手椅上。

“埃莉，这是一个朋友，他在帮安妮料理些家里的事。我来煮些咖啡。”

“你知道吗？”我边环顾四周边说，“你们在这下边住了个好地方，比我在昆斯区住的地方要好。你们一直住在这下边吗？”我问道。

第32页

“当然了。”埃莉回答道，“这里冬暖夏凉，而且我们不用付房租。”

“你们在下边安全吗？”

“我们在大街上住过。”利昂娜说，“我可以告诉你，地下更安全。这里的每个人都互相认识。如果有陌生人进来，我们便会知道。地铁工人知道我们，他们不管我们。”

利昂娜开始挪动成堆的黑色塑料袋，下面有一个上了锁的旧金属盒子。

“纳特，”她说，“安妮想让你把这个盒子带给她。”

利昂娜把我带回到街道上。在回市区第 28 街的路上，我在想我在地铁上途经了多少个那样的地下社区。

回到医院后，我把盒子交给安妮。然后她拿出系在她脖子上的钥匙，打开盒子，给我看了一张开心的少年的照片。

“纳特，”安妮说，“这是我的儿子，杰基。我已经 20 年没见过他了，我想请你找到他。”

“我从来不知道你有家人。”我说。

“你并不了解我的全部。我可能活不了多久了，纳特，我希望在我死之前见到他。我们过去住在布朗克斯南部的国民住宅。那儿不是个好地方。离开家之后，杰基曾经时不时地回去看看。通常是回去借钱。我知道他不是个好孩子，但他是我的儿子。他爸爸是高管，我曾在他的办公室当清洁工。他是那种会跟每个女人说自己的妻子不懂他的人。我当时空虚寂寞，然后我们就好上了。他让我开怀大笑，而杰基就是我们俩好上的结果。”

第33页

“他现在多大？”我问道。

“他 1954 年出生，所以跟你差不多大。”安妮说，“我最后一次见他是 1979 年在赖克斯岛监狱。他一直偷车，还总打架。在布朗克斯这个地方很容易交到不好的朋友。我到监狱探视他时，他说他再也不想见到我，这伤透了我的心。从那一刻起，我的生活四分五裂。我感觉十分低落，从那时起我开始在曼哈顿街头流浪。我必须逃离，离开布朗克斯，并且忘记这些。”

“你还有其他能告诉我的吗？”我问道。

“我曾经听说他住在下东区，”她说，“是一名出租车司机。”

“你是说一名出租车司机？如果他有案底，他没办法找到出租车司机这种工作。他的全名是？”

第34页

“杰基 · 罗宾森 · 克莱顿。”

“身高？”我问道。

“大约五英尺十英寸。”安妮虚弱地说，“哦，他在他的左臂上文了一只鸟，美国之鹰。如果你找到他，告诉他他的妈妈想见他。带他来这里，这很重要。”

“我会尽力的，安妮。”我说，“但是你别抱太大希望，这可能很困难。”

安妮把照片交给我，然后锁上了盒子。接着她让我把盒子和钥匙带到威尔玛 · 帕特森的办公室。她躺回到床上，浑身冒汗，呼吸沉重。我叫了护士，安妮看起来奄奄一息。

第 5 章　内部消息

第35页

我在午饭时到了麦克法登酒吧。里面虽然喧嚣吵闹、人头攒动，但因为有空调十分凉爽。我感觉饿了，从前一天早饭后我就没正经吃过东西。我点了牛排，另加了薯条。我正吃饭的时候，酒保杰克叫了我。

“嘿，纳特，这里有个兄弟说你会请他喝一杯。”我抬起头。埃德·温切斯特正向我挥舞一个空酒杯。

"好吧，我想我会的。"我说，"来这儿，埃德。最好是个重磅消息。"

"我喜欢这么做买卖。"埃德说，"你请我喝酒，我帮你找消息。"

埃德告诉我他去了《每日新闻》图书馆，读了所有关于惠特克航空的内容，故事很精彩。汤姆·惠特克是个有趣的家伙。他曾是一名美国空军飞行员，第一次世界大战时在法国被击落。他是少数几个有幸活着回来的人员之一。从空军退伍之后，他买了几架退役飞机，然后开始载着乘客环游城市，空中观光。在 20 世纪 20 年代末期，他开了一家航空公司，经营飞往华盛顿和芝加哥的航班。他看出未来将会是航空旅行的时代。在 20 世纪 50 年代，铁路客源开始流失到航空公司，惠特克航空占据了很大的份额。

第36页

"他是那种为工作而活的人吗？"我问道。

"完全不是，"埃德答道，"他是个招蜂引蝶的家伙。看看这个，1957 年的《每日新闻》。"

埃德给了我一份新闻报道的复印件，上面是汤姆·惠特克和三位明艳动人的金发美女在一家鸡尾酒酒吧的桌边。每个美女的身材和长相都比玛丽莲·梦露还要好。惠特克看起来怡然自得。我能明白为什么。

"看看他，"埃德说，"他可能是你的兄弟。"

"我们可能长得像，"我说，"但是他所拥有的一切我都没有，钱和女人。"

埃德接着告诉我，汤姆·惠特克工作努力，玩儿得也疯狂。即便是结婚后，他也和其他女人暧昧不清。那并不是一段美满的婚姻，他和惠特克夫人很可能是为了孩子们才在一起的。20 世纪 60 年代末，他把惠特克航空卖给了泛美航空。之后他大部分时间都在锡蒂岛，喝酒、钓鱼。他 1974 年去世。

第37页

“永别了，汤姆 · 惠特克。”我说。

“你走运了，兄弟。”埃德说，“她死后，你就能请所有人喝酒了。”

我步行回到东 43 街。我到办公室的时候，斯特拉正在电脑前忙碌着。

“嗨，斯特拉，”我说，“我刚跟埃德聊天了。”

“你是指聊天和喝酒吧？”斯特拉回答说。

“是啊。和埃德打交道，这两者缺一不可。”

我告诉了斯特拉从埃德那里了解到的所有内容。

“你知道吗，纳特，这吓到我了——惠特克夫人、玛莎、那间公寓。”她说。

“嗯，就像恐怖电影里的东西。”

“你说对了，”斯特拉补充道，“想象一下从不出门，那是种什么生活？惠特克夫人脑子不正常。”

“如果她把钱留给我的话，确实不正常。”我说，“有什么我要见的客户吗？”

“电话一整天都没有响过。”斯特拉说。

“哦，好吧。我要去世纪公寓见一个我在那儿认识的不疯的人，看门人鲍勃。”

第38页

我到了世纪公寓，走进大厅。空调运转得非常好，仿佛走进了 12 月。

“鲍勃，记得我吗？”我问道。

“啊，马利先生。”他说。

“叫我纳特吧。我想问你几个关于惠特克夫人的问题。”

“现在，马利先生……纳特，”他说，“我真的不应该谈论我们的……”

“这个有用吗？”我问道。

我向他出示我的侦探执照，有点儿帮助。我又拿出一张50美元的钞票给他看，这帮了大忙。

“哎呀，谢谢你。”他说。

“惠特克夫人怎么得到她需要的每样东西？”我问。

“玛莎会去买一些东西，或者商店把东西送到公寓。惠特克夫人是那种喜欢被照顾的类型。”

“经常会有人来拜访她吗？”

“我来这儿五年了。”鲍勃说，“在这期间，我见过的访客只有她的儿子和女儿，尽管他们只来过这里三四次。上一次我看到他们还是两年多以前。我还记得是因为他们离开时都气冲冲的，女儿还哭了。家庭分歧或者什么的。”

第39页

所以惠特克夫人除了玛莎之外见不到任何人，我想。这不是一种健康的生活方式。

第6章　东村

第40页

办公室的电梯时不时就会坏掉，今天就坏了。爬了八层楼之后，我觉得又热又不舒服。风扇根本不起什么作用。秋天也不能很快来临。

我要打几个电话。最后，真正的工作是寻找一个失踪者——安妮的儿子，杰基。我的第一个电话要打给警察局总部。我认识一个能帮上忙的人，我过去曾和他共过事。更确切地说，当他情绪不是那么糟糕的时候。

“帮我找一下奥尔登伯格警监，可以吗？”

“马利！”奥尔登伯格喊道，“你不给我打电话我的问题就已经够多的了。”

“听起来你的工作不太顺心。”我说，“听着，我正在找一个失踪的人，他叫杰基·罗宾森·克莱顿。他曾经犯过事，1979 年被关在赖克斯岛监狱。他现在可能在当出租车司机，46 岁，中等个头儿，左臂上文了一只美国鹰。”

“还有别的吗？”奥尔登伯格问道。

第41页

“没了。”我说，“他母亲已经有 20 年没见过他了。另外，奥尔登伯格，这是在为一个老朋友办事。”

“好的，马利。”奥尔登伯格说，“但是这大热天我不会动一根手指头，我让布兰德斯坦警督去做。”

“首先，”我说，“让他查一下这家伙是否在监狱，行吗？”

接下来我需要一些来自《每日新闻》的消息。我给埃德·温切斯特打了个电话。很幸运，他从麦克法登酒吧回去了。

“纳特，我能为你做什么？”他问道。

“我正在找一个叫杰基·罗宾森·克莱顿的家伙。”我说，“他犯过事，所以也许会有关于他的新闻报道。”

我给了埃德他需要的信息。我交叉着手指，希望他能发现些什么。

我刚一挂断电话，铃声就响了。布兰德斯坦警督办事漂亮，杰基·克莱顿不在美国的任何监狱中。我们进展顺利，我开始觉得高兴。这才是一个私家侦探该有的生活。我甚至忘记了天气有多么炎热。现在我需要一些额外的帮助，乔·布兰尼正是合适的人选。他以前是个警察，五大三粗的，有时帮我做事。

第42页

"乔，我是纳特。听着，我现在的生活里都是老太太。我有一个奇怪的客户——一位叫乔安娜·惠特克的夫人。还有和她住在一起的玛莎，她甚至更加古怪。我需要知道更多关于她们的信息。"我告诉乔到目前为止发生了什么，并且给了他地址和具体的描述。

"老大，"乔说，"你确实遇见了几个疯子！"

第二天早上我在下东区溜达，试图找到杰基。通常，你翻开一块石头时，会在石头下面发现一些令人不快的东西。家庭也是如此，你查明得越多，就会发现越多不堪。我希望这不会发生在杰基身上。

我走访了几家出租车公司和酒吧，都不走运。当你找一个四十多岁的人，用的却是一张他十几岁时候的照片，能有什么进展呢？最终，我在唐人街的运河大街上找到了一名听说过杰基的出租车司机。他告诉我去东村试试。

我从 A、B、C 大道找起，这里曾以字母城著称。开始完全是浪费时间，直到我到达 B 大道的瓦扎克酒吧。

我给酒保看了杰基的照片。我跟他说起文身的时候，我能看出他听说过杰基。他恶狠狠地看了我一眼。

第43页

“你是警察吗？”他问道。

“不是，哥们儿，”我说，“我叫马利，只是一个本分的私家侦探。”

我给他看了我的执照。

“我不和警察或者私家侦探打交道，先生。”酒保说。

“你这里真不错，很友好。客人会觉得自己很受欢迎。你和钱打交道吗？”

我把执照翻过来，背面是一张 20 美元的钞票。酒保伸手去够钱的时候，我把手抽开了。

“没这么快。你知道些什么？”我问道。

“好吧，我认识他。”他说，“最近没见到他。他有钱，但不是开出租车赚的。”

“哦，是吗？”我说，“那么钱都是从哪儿来的呢？”

“买别人偷来的东西。”他回答说，“如果你有什么好东西，去找杰基。但别惹他生气——他很凶。”

“你知道他为谁工作吗？”我问道。

“我现在能拿到我的 20 美元了吗？”

“告诉我他为谁工作。”我说。

第44页

“去 A 大道的怀斯曼出租车公司打听试试，”酒保说，“就在汤普金斯广场公园以外的住宅区。”

我把 20 美元的钞票放在吧台上，然后走了出去。我很熟悉汤普金斯广场公园。我当巡警的时候，这个公园曾是东村大多数流浪者的家。他们过去把这个社区叫作“帐篷城市”。后来，他们被责令离开，但并不是没有发生冲突，随后这个地方被清理干净了。我找到了那家出租车公司。有几辆出租车停在外面，我假装成游客。桌边的那个家伙凶狠地瞪了我一眼。

“你能帮我一下吗，先生？”我问道，“我正在度假，我是第一次来纽约。我想租一天出租车，能好好地观光一下。”

桌子后边的家伙看上去仿佛很多天没有睡觉、洗漱和刮胡子了。他身上的味道比我的还要难闻。他点了一支烟，然后咳嗽了足足 15 秒钟。终于，他能说话了。

“先生，我们今天不租车。”他说。

“嘿，”我说，“这不是家出租车公司吗？”

“我再说一遍，我们不租车。你是不是傻？”

有一件事显而易见，怀斯曼出租车公司并不需要顾客，当然是不需要那种想要租车的顾客。他们有另一条业务线，我想知道是什么。我决定出其不意试探他。

第45页

“怀斯曼先生？”我问。

“你怎么知道我的名字？”

“可能是外边的牌子告诉我的。”我回答完继续说，“我正在找杰基·克莱顿。”

“哦，是吗？”他说，“你找他做什么？”

“是私事，家务事。”我说。

“哦，恰巧我也正在找他，等我找到他，我要……”他停住了，就像他说了不该说的话。

“你要做什么？”我问。

“滚出这里！”怀斯曼嚷嚷道，“我不知道我为什么要跟你说话。

别再到这儿来多管闲事！”

我觉得我已经不再招人待见。我离开后用手机给乔·布兰尼打了电话。

“我是纳特。今天早上过得怎么样，乔？”

“很好。就是和惠特克夫人喝了咖啡，吃了蛋糕。”

“你是怎么做到的，乔？”

“简单。我认识一个在东28街开花店的家伙。我买了一些花，附上一张纸条，写着‘来自你特别的朋友纳特·马利’。然后我借了他店里的衣服，假装我是花店的人，用这种方式来到了公寓。我刚一说花是马利先生送的，这位老太太就打开了话匣子。她认为你特别好。”

第46页

“我知道，”我说，“这让人烦恼，不是吗？”

“然后我让惠特克夫人谈谈她的家人。她想着她死去的丈夫的那个世界。我试图让她谈谈孩子们，但是她只是说他们再也不会来了。我在门厅桌子上的通讯录里找到了她儿子的电话号码，小菜一碟。”

“干得好，乔。现在，我有另外一项工作。我想让你监视A大道上的怀斯曼出租车公司，杰基为他们工作过。那儿正发生一些奇怪的事。他们不让我租出租车，所以我想知道他们怎么赚钱。要弄到一些照片。”

乔给了我查利·惠特克单位和家里的电话号码。也许威尔玛·帕特森可以让惠特克一家谈谈。我给她办公室打电话告诉了她电话号码，傍晚时分她给我回了电话。

第47页

“纳特？我是威尔玛。我跟查利·惠特克谈过了。他说他们过去曾带着孩子们去探望，但后来那成了一件十分痛苦的事情。惠特克夫人不断提起她死去的丈夫，而且说的时候仿佛他是神一样。真实情况是那是一段没有爱的婚姻，汤姆从来没有时间陪伴孩子。实际上，查利说父亲对他们而言像个陌生人。”

“这是一种什么样的成长方式啊。”我说。

“查利·惠特克已经同意试着安排一次家庭会面。”威尔玛继续说道，“他妈妈拒绝和他通电话，所以他只能亲自去拜访。这一切都需要时间。况且她会同意吗？这令人怀疑。”

“好吧，这真是一团糟！”我说。

“别自责了，纳特。”

第 7 章　进展

第48页

这是漫长的一天。差不多是时候喝杯冰镇啤酒了。斯特拉正在她的办公桌前读东西。

“事情进展如何，斯特拉？”我问道。

“一切都好，除了办公室太热。”斯特拉答道，“我没法儿工作，我头疼。”

“消息收到。所以一切正常，”我说，“这是我想听到的。你在读什么呢？”

“空调机组。你知道它们是什么——能使房间凉爽起来的智能机器。”她举起其中一个的照片。

“继续做梦吧！这些东西费钱。”我说。

电话响了，是乔。

“纳特？我整个下午一直在监视怀斯曼出租车公司，那间办公室总有人进进出出。出租车司机进去时拎着一个手提箱，出来时拎着另外一个，然后开车离开。看起来除了载客什么都做。”

“有意思。我想知道怀斯曼到底在忙什么。”

第49页

“答案在那些箱子里，老大。”

“你拍到照片了吗？”我问。

“用了整整一卷儿胶卷呢，现在正在冲洗。”乔答道。

“做得好，一杯写着你名字的冰啤会在麦克法登酒吧等你。”

为什么要花钱去蒸桑拿呢？只需要坐在办公室里流汗就够了。也许斯特拉是对的，她在很多事情上通常都是对的。我正想着冰啤的时候，费希尔医生从贝尔维尤医院打来电话，安妮的情况正在恶化。

“她还能再坚持多久，医生？”我问。

“她患心脏病已经很多年了，加上在车站那次心脏病发作……我非常担心，马利先生。”

“她还清醒吗？”

“是的，不过是刚醒来。”

“好吧，我有一些消息应该可以让她坚持住。”我说，“我们正在找她的儿子，而且已经有眉目了。我们在东村找到了他之前的老板，他们之间似乎有一些争执。我猜测杰基正在躲着他。就告诉她我们快找到了。”

第50页

放下电话，我感觉既悲伤又气恼。为那些不得不住在街上的人感到悲伤，对这个迫使他们在街上过活的社会感到气恼。

斯特拉抬起头来不读了。

“怎么了，纳特？”

“是安妮。如果我们不快点儿找到杰基，等不到见他她就会死了。”我说。

“纳特，我有个主意。”

“嗯？”

“我给黄页上的每家出租车公司打电话怎么样？我可以说我是杰基的前女友，想要再见他一面，好好谈谈。”斯特拉说。

“好主意。但是首先，我需要一些吃的和啤酒。你锁好门之后，咱们在麦克法登酒吧见。”

《每日新闻》的埃德·温切斯特正看着我喝完第一杯啤酒。啤酒凉爽可口，几乎没触碰到我的喉咙两侧就下去了。我瞬间觉得好多了。

“纳特，你也太渴了吧！现在，我有些消息要告诉你。是《每日新闻》上五年前的消息。但是首先……”

“我了解，我得再花一杯酒的钱才能听这个故事。这故事最好有意思。”

埃德递给我一份新闻报道的复印件，标题写着《韦斯曼和克莱顿无罪》。我接着读下去。“厄恩斯特·韦斯曼和杰基·克莱顿在被判没有构成买卖赃物罪之后，于今日释放。”

第51页

“这就对了。”我说，“乔花了一个下午的时间盯着怀斯曼出租车公司的动静。杰基·克莱顿过去在怀斯曼出租车公司做事。在这篇报道里，杰基和一个叫韦斯曼的家伙在一起。也许他改了名字，为了听上去更像美国人。”

第52页

乔带着照片到了，是一张又一张出租车司机拿着不同手提箱进出办公室的照片，还有一张极令人满意的怀斯曼的照片。

“就是他，”我说，“现在如果我们把他和《每日新闻》上厄恩斯特·韦斯曼的照片比较一下。是的，是同一个人。而且他年纪大了却一点儿也没变好看。这是纽约市警察局的工作。抱歉，我要给奥尔登伯格警监打个电话。”

奥尔登伯格心情不好，他听起来好像马上要大发雷霆了。这很正常，也很自然，他心情好的时候我反而有些担忧。

第53页

“你想要什么，马利？别浪费我的时间。”

“奥尔登伯格，你记得一个叫韦斯曼的家伙吗？大约五年前他被判无罪。”

“记得，我真想再抓他一回。”

“你可能会梦想成真。找几个你的手下去监视A大道上的怀斯曼出租车公司。我觉得韦斯曼，他现在化名为怀斯曼，还干着同样的勾当，他用出租车生意当幌子。”

“这听起来有戏，马利。”

“你要是抓到了韦斯曼，狠狠地收拾他。”

“相信我，马利。你跟他有什么过节？”奥尔登伯格问道。

“他不让我租车。”

我从在纽约市警察局那个时候开始就知道奥尔登伯格是我遇到过的最难相处的人之一。奇怪的是我喜欢这个家伙。只要你和他站在同一阵营，一切都好说。

还有一杯啤酒在酒吧里等着我呢，我总是和啤酒走得很近。

第54页

“奥尔登伯格怎么说？”乔问。

“他正在气头上。”我答道。

“那有什么新消息？”

斯特拉到了，还拿来了另一本空调杂志。她给我看封面，上面写着：“七月你也可以保持凉爽、清新、悠然自在。南极空调，帮你挥别夏日忧愁。两台空调机组，仅售不到700美元。”

不到700美元？价格是699。这让我的体温上升，但是我知道我输了。如果这能让斯特拉高兴，那也值了。

“就它吧！你赢了，斯特拉。在我改变主意之前赶紧行动吧。”我说。

“什么情况，老大？”乔问道。

“纳特仁慈地同意了为办公室装空调。”斯特拉说。

我将损失700美元，这真的让我很伤心，就像失去了一位密友一样。看来惠特克夫人的2000美元还没打入我的银行账户，我就要开始花了。

第8章　家人去世

第55页

那天晚上我努力想睡一会儿觉。我记起听说过的一个方法。用一台电风扇，在一个碗里放大量冰，把风扇放在碗的后边，打开电风扇，等待凉爽的空气。按理应该是这样的。开始有一点儿小小的改善，但后来冰化成了水。这并没有坚持很长时间，而我也没有多余的冰了，又是一个不眠之夜。在凌晨三点的时候我放弃了。我可以选择疲惫不堪地待在家里，或者是疲惫不堪地去办公室。但至少半夜去上班的路上会凉快些。

纽约地铁从不停运。而且自从市长整顿清理之后，城市变得安全了很多。我并不担心在这个时候乘坐地铁。凌晨四点钟，曼哈顿市中心感觉像是另一座城市。街上几乎一个人也没有，连空气闻起来都是新鲜的。到了办公室，我打开窗户和所有风扇。终于，我睡着了。早上八点，斯特拉发现我还在睡。

第56页

“纳特！”她喊道，“你喝酒了吗？”

“实话实说，斯特拉，”我迷迷糊糊地说，“我在家睡不着。我想你睡得很好吧？”

“我总是睡得很好。出去给自己买点儿早饭吧，纳特。顺便帮我带回一杯咖啡，可以吗？”

在外面，我已经能够感受到从人行道上升腾起来的热气。20分钟后我带着咖啡和甜甜圈回来了。走路对我并没有什么好处。现在斯特拉把四台电风扇都搬进了她的办公室里吹着。

“嘿！我现在连一台风扇也没有了？”我问道。

“把它们拿走吧，纳特。”斯特拉说道，“我只是在你出去的时候借用了你的两台风扇。费希尔医生传来了安妮的消息，跟昨天晚上的情况一样。”

“她是个斗士，”我说，“在为杰基坚持着。”

电话响了，我没听出是谁的声音。

“马利先生吗？我是世纪公寓的比安奇小姐，就是你知道的玛莎，那个听人差遣的女人。嗯，现在开始我不需要再听从任何差遣了。老太太去世了。”

“哦？”我说，“你还好吗，玛莎？”

“我当然很好。”她说，“但她不好，她身子已经凉了。”

“我马上就到。”我告诉她。

第57页

事情发展得太快了，不是我所希望的。我转向斯特拉。“惠特克夫人去世了。关上事务所，我们一起过去看看。”

在世纪公寓，看门人鲍勃和我一样惊讶，这是他刚听说惠特克夫人的死讯。他给楼上公寓打了电话，两分钟后我们到了门前。这一次我们很快就进去了。随后，又一件令人惊讶的事：玛莎在笑。

“告诉我发生了什么？”我问道。

“当然可以。”玛莎说，“我端着惠特克夫人的早茶进去，她就在那儿，浑身冰凉，已经死了。来看看。”

“我待在这儿就好。”斯特拉用手捂住嘴说。

惠特克夫人在她的床上。她的嘴和眼睛都张得大大的，皮肤发灰，她已经死了。

“摸摸她，”玛莎边抬起惠特克夫人纤细的手臂边说，“她身子已经凉了。”

“我相信你的话，玛莎。不过别再碰尸体了。医生已经给她检查过了吗？”

“为什么要检查呢？现在医生也无能为力了。”

“什么？打电话叫医生，现在！”

第58页

玛莎走出房间去打电话的时候，我迅速环顾四周。床头柜上有一瓶药片。帮助她睡眠的？我会查一下。其他所有东西看起来都完全正常。我有查利·惠特克的号码，我让斯特拉打电话告诉他这个消息。她处理这种事会比我做得好。

医生到来之前，我需要问玛莎几个问题。我在厨房找到她，她的一双大脚搭在桌子上，正读着一本旧侦探小说，还听着收音机里的乡村音乐。我关掉了收音机。

“嘿！你为什么要这么做？”她质问道。

“玛莎，”我说，“我们得聊聊。”

“聊什么？”

“你觉得呢？当然是惠特克夫人。你最后见到惠特克夫人活着是什么时候？”我问道。

“我给她端进去热巧克力的时候，”玛莎说，“昨天晚上十点。”

“你通常都要给惠特克夫人药片吗？”

“当然了。睡前两片帮助她睡觉。”玛莎答道。

“那么昨天晚上和其他每天晚上都一样吗？”我问道。

“是的，为什么会不一样呢？”她说，“你为什么问我这些问题？”

第59页

“这是我的工作。你今天早上什么时候发现她的？”

“和平常一样的时间。”玛莎回答。

“好的，”我耐心地说，“不过那是几点？”

“八点一刻。她就在那儿，浑身冰凉。”

我环顾厨房。“你没碰她屋子里的任何东西吧？”

“没有，先生，”玛莎边向我挥舞着她的书边说，“我从侦探小说里知道的，不要碰任何东西。”

但她碰了，那个热巧克力的杯子已经被洗过了。我知道有什么地方不对劲。玛莎兴高采烈，她看起来很享受每一刻。医生到了，我没时间担心更多的事情了。斯特拉带他进来。

“纳特，这是休斯医生。”她说。

“很高兴见到你，”我说，“我叫马利。我在为惠特克夫人做事。玛莎打电话告诉了我这个消息。”

医生进入卧室做检查，以确定惠特克夫人的死因。几分钟后，我敲门进入卧室找他。医生已经用床单将她盖住。

“说实话，马利先生，我已经料到会这样了。”医生说，“她心脏不好已经有一段时间了，是自然死亡。我现在就开具死亡证明。已经告知她家人了吗？”

第60页

“我刚告诉了她的儿子。”斯特拉回答说，“查利·惠特克已在路上。”

“很好。现在必须尽快把尸体送到殡仪馆，显然这家人会安排那些事情。”休斯医生说。

整个情形让我感觉不舒服。有些事不对劲，但是我没法儿说出到底是什么事。玛莎站得很近，听着每一个字。我得把她支开一会儿。

“玛莎，给每个人都来杯咖啡。另外我的早餐咖啡总是配巧克力碎曲奇一起吃。”我说。

“我们没有巧克力碎曲奇。”玛莎说。

“给你五美元。去买一些，可以吗？”

玛莎离开时，休斯医生和斯特拉看上去有点儿吃惊。

“这应该会花上她十分钟时间。”我说。

“纳特，为什么要让玛莎去买东西呢？”斯特拉问道。

“在我看来，玛莎太高兴了。”我说，“而且我不想让她听到医生说的每句话。她的行为很奇怪，她笑的时候让我觉得很紧张。惠特克夫人定期吃安眠药吗，医生？”

第61页

“是的。我建议她服用安眠药，”医生回答，“她一直有失眠的困扰。”

“能请你看看这个瓶子吗？”我问。

我和医生一起走进卧室。

“数量看起来是对的。”他说，“她每月有一瓶新的。不过，马利先生，你应该不会认为……”

“我也不知道该怎么认为，医生。这是问题所在。”我说。

“你看，马利先生，”休斯医生说，“惠特克夫人是一位有心脏病的老妇人，她的去世并不意外。好了，给你一份死亡证明。这里没有什么我能做的了。有人要和玛莎一起在这里等吗？”

“我会等，医生，”我说，“谢谢。”

我觉得我不应该让玛莎单独和尸体待在一起。我等的时候，斯特拉有工作可以做。

“我们两个人都在这儿待着没有意义。”我对斯特拉说，“你能先回办公室给那些出租车公司打电话吗？我们得找到杰基，而且要快。”

过了一会儿，玛莎带着曲奇回来了。她狠狠地瞪了我一眼。

第62页

“嗯！我的最爱。”我说，“你煮好咖啡后过来坐下跟我聊聊你自己。”

这没有意义。我觉得即便是奥尔登伯格警监也无法从她身上得到任何信息。我从她口中得到的最多信息便是简单的“是”“不是”或者“不知道”。不管怎么说，在我等待查利过来的时候这帮我打发了时间。我真的想到街上去找杰基。

第 9 章　找到失踪的儿子

第63页

刚过中午，查利·惠特克到了世纪公寓。我无意中让他受到了不愉快的惊吓。

“我的天！你吓死我了！所以你是纳特·马利？”他满脸惊讶地说，“你可能是我爸爸的鬼魂，这让我想起了那些不美好的记忆，他过去检查我作业的样子。如果我十道题里对的少于八个就会挨打。”

“那么我希望外貌是我和你父亲唯一的相似之处。”我说，“我对你母亲的事情感到很难过，惠特克先生。”

“谢谢，”查利伤心地说，“但我们多少也料到了会如此。”

我让玛莎去厨房再准备一些咖啡，然后带着查利进入卧室。他掀开床单，站在那里若有所思地看着。

“好吧，再见，妈妈。”他最终说道。

第64页

“我知道现在不是时候，但是我们能聊聊吗？”我问，“威尔玛·帕特森已经解释了遗嘱的情况。我想说我从没同意过那份遗嘱。我跟威尔玛说要将所有东西都还给你们家——钱、公寓，还有其他的。我只需要签署一些文件。”我说。

“谢谢，被卷入这件事情不是你的错。”

“我担心玛莎，”我说，“她的行为非常奇怪。”

“我不记得她的行为什么时候不奇怪。”查利说，“你不用待在这里，现在我能料理这里所有的事。”

“这是我的名片。如果有任何我能帮忙的，打电话给我。”

惠特克家的事占据了很多宝贵的时间，我们并没有很多时间。回到东43街，斯特拉还在给各家出租车公司打电话。

“哦，你好。我在想你是否能帮到我？不知道有没有一个叫杰基·克莱顿的司机在你那里上班，嗯？没有？还是要谢谢你。”

她挂了电话。

“纳特，”她说，“这是第50家出租车公司。我们最终会找到的。”

第65页

“干得好，斯特拉。如果有必要的话，也打电话给斯塔滕岛和布鲁克林吧。”

她还没来得及继续打，电话响了。有人在电话另一头大喊大叫。斯特拉举着电话伸直了胳膊，是奥尔登伯格警监。

“奥尔登伯格，事情进展如何？”我问。

“我一上午都想要打通你的电话，你的电话一直占线。”奥尔登伯格以他常用的直接方式回应。“谢谢你关于怀斯曼的消息。我的手下搜查了他的地方，你该看看我们在那儿找到的东西。他要在监狱待很长时间。”

“听着，奥尔登伯格，我需要和怀斯曼聊聊。”

我解释了我们多么需要找到杰基·克莱顿，以便让他见见他奄奄一息的母亲。

“你当然可以跟他聊，但是他会跟你聊吗？”警监问道。

我乘坐4号线特快列车到市中心，很快就穿越曼哈顿到了警察局大厦，速度比任何一辆出租车都快。奥尔登伯格警监正在警察局总部等我，然后带我去了牢房。这让我想起我在纽约市警察局的那些年。怀斯曼还是一贯地自我感觉良好。他的身体状况看上去比惠特克夫人还要糟。

第66页

“怀斯曼先生，你记得我吗？纳特·马利，私家侦探。我需要你的帮助。我必须在杰基·克莱顿的母亲死之前找到他。”

“如果我能抓到他，我要把他撕成碎片。”怀斯曼回答说。

“我确信你很有想法，但是那帮不上我什么忙。”

“我和杰基是搭档，不过他离开我并且破坏了我们的约定。我们都清楚，不和我一起他哪儿也去不了。离我远点儿，我不和私家侦探说话，你们这种人让我恶心。”

至少我知道了一些事情，杰基正试图逃避他的过去。也许我们抓到他的时候，他会同意去看他妈妈。现在是下午三点左右。我给斯特拉打了电话，看看她给出租车公司打电话有什么进展。

“纳特？”她说，“我们有发现。在西 14 街的帕特尔出租车公司，我甚至还和他说了话。但他只是说‘我没有什么前女友’，说完就挂了电话。”

“这是乔·布兰尼的工作，”我说，“让他盯着那个地方。你能把地址给我吗？”

“第九大道第 14 街。”斯特拉说，“你知道，就是所有肉类加工厂所在的地方。”

第67页

“好的。告诉乔我会在那儿跟他会面。”

我到那里的时候，乔已经就位了。他坐在自己的车里，把帽子拉下来遮住眼睛，看起来像个正在睡觉的家伙。但我知道他正关注着那条街上每一个细小的举动。下午晚些时候，肉类加工商们已经下班了。我们停在一架旧铁路桥下方的两辆巨型卡车中间。帕特尔出租车公司在街对面向北一点儿。这可能会耗费很长时间。我们盯着，等待着。出租车来来往往，但是没有杰基的踪影。几个小时过去了，我们慢慢地在热浪中被煎烤着。终于，我看到他了。

“他在那儿，乔。”我说。

杰基变了，他不再是报纸照片上那个凶狠的家伙。他看起来就像任何一个在做着自己正当职业的正常人一样。我跑到马路对面，喊道：“杰基·克莱顿！我们聊聊你母亲的事。”

他并没有停下来听我说话。我刚说到“杰基”，他就像一个受到惊吓的人一样跑了起来，而且他比我快得多。我们在两个工厂之间的狭窄入口处跟丢了他。当然，他比我们更熟悉那个地方。我们束手无策。我们最后的机会是去问帕特尔出租车公司。接待员并不希望看到我们。

第68页

“你看，”她对我们说，“杰基说不管是谁到这儿来问问题，我什么都不要说。”

“谢谢，女士，”我说，“意思我明白了。”

晚上八点，我又累又热又饿。

“今天我们没有什么可做的了，乔。”

我用自己的手机打了几个电话。我让斯特拉回家，然后让费希尔医生给安妮带个消息。如果安妮知道我们看到了杰基，也许会帮她坚持下去。

我们穿过第八大道，往城郊方向走三个街区有一家古巴中餐馆，那里的鸡肉饭做得很棒，更重要的是那里有冰镇啤酒。那让我感觉好一点儿，但是我仍然觉得没有用。

“乔，我们就差一点儿。现在杰基遇到任何陌生人都会紧张。”我说。

“你也无能为力，老大。”乔说。

“但是我们还有一个机会，奥尔登伯格。我们帮助他找到怀斯曼，所以他欠我们点儿东西。他能给我们杰基的地址。纽约市出租车和轿车委员会掌握着市里所有出租车司机的信息。那些信息是保密的，但对纽约市警察局并不保密。”

第69页

我给警察局总部打了电话。幸运的是，奥尔登伯格还在楼里。

“你无家可归吗，奥尔登伯格？”我问道。

“马利，我的孩子十几岁，警察局总部更清静。”他大笑着说。

“我把怀斯曼交给了你，所以我觉得你欠我的。我需要一个出租车司机的地址，他的名字是杰基·克莱顿，我跟你提到过，他给西 14 街帕特尔出租车公司开车。尽快，奥尔登伯格，他妈妈奄奄一息了。”

“我尽力而为，”他说，“但是在明天之前我什么都不能保证。你需要查资料的办公室现在已经下班了。”

我们能做的只有等待。

第 10 章　我们是好人

第70页

我讨厌汗水让衬衫粘在地铁车座上的感觉。这么热的天我每天要换三四件干净的衬衫。今天早上我需要一件清爽的衬衫，但是没有时间换了。查利·惠特克和威尔玛·帕特森正在办公室里等着呢。

"马利先生，谢天谢地你终于来了！"查利说，"我想请你和我们一起去趟公寓，我会在出租车上解释。玛莎失踪了。"

"好的，我们走。斯特拉，奥尔登伯格一打电话你就往世纪公寓打电话给我。"

在出租车上，查利·惠特克解释了发生的事情。"我母亲已经被送到殡仪馆。我和帕特森夫人约定好今天早上第一件事是在公寓见面，开始详细研究我母亲的文件。我昨晚住在一家酒店，我不想住在那间公寓。我们早上七点半到那里，发现那里乱七八糟，东西全都散落在地板上。最初我以为是入室抢劫，但是玛莎的房间没有被碰过。我觉得这有点儿蹊跷。"

第71页

"丢了什么东西吗？"我问道。

"还不清楚，马利先生。这是我希望你能帮忙的地方。你能查出究竟发生了什么，并且找到玛莎吗？我只是觉得有些事情非常不对劲。"

惠特克公寓里，书和文件被扔得到处都是，家具和玻璃的碎片散落在地毯上。沙发和扶手椅上到处都是割痕，填充的东西也被拽了出来。厨房的地板是湿的，油、牛奶和酒正慢慢地跟成袋的面粉和糖混在一起。一瓶打碎的番茄酱放在满是洗发水的浴盆里。马桶里是撕成碎片的惠特克夫妇的结婚照片。

"现在看看玛莎的房间。"查利说。

这个小巧简单的卧室干净整洁。没有手提箱，看起来她仿佛带走了她的大部分东西。书架上全都是侦探故事：雷蒙德·钱德勒、埃勒里·奎因、埃德·麦克贝恩。在镜子上，她用口红写着："去玩儿球了。"

"这个神秘的信息是什么意思？"威尔玛问。

第72页

“我还不确定，但肯定是玛莎干的。”我答道。

“现在怎么办？”查利问。

“找出所有没有被拿走的东西——钱、支票簿和信用卡。我们需要弄清楚丢了什么。别让这房间看起来像是已经被你翻过的。在警察来之前，我们实际上不应该碰任何东西。”

“警察？我们必须要找警察吗？”查利问。

“惠特克先生，谋杀案是警察的事。”

“你不会真的认为玛莎……”

“这正是我所想的。我知道有些事情一直不太对劲。”

“我说什么呢？”查利问道。

“说有谋杀案，你电话还没挂掉他们就会赶到这里。对了惠特克先生，在你打 911 之前，现在先给殡仪馆打电话。告诉他们不要碰你母亲的遗体。如果他们正在为葬礼而修整遗体，告诉他们立刻停止。警察会仔细查看你母亲的尸体以确定她的死因。应该会立即进行尸检。”

在警察到来之前，我们有时间快速查看一圈。没有支票簿、现金或是信用卡的踪影。纽约市警察局的警队不到十分钟就赶到了公寓。

第73页

斯特拉打来电话。

“纳特？我们拿到了杰基的地址，在切尔西 · 阿姆斯酒店。在第八大道和第 22 街的拐角处附近。”

“在切尔西，嗯？我们昨天晚上经过了那里。接下来做这些，给医院打电话，传消息给安妮，说我们知道杰基住在哪儿了。然后看看杰基是否在工作。假装你是出租车和轿车委员会的，说一位乘客记下了克莱顿先生的号码并且投诉了他，你想和他聊聊。这样你能查出他什么时候上下班。回电话到这里找我。”

威尔玛带着案发现场小组的警督走过来。

“我们已经查看过了，先生。”他说，“目前还没有任何东西被偷的迹象。惠特克先生，能告诉我你母亲以前在哪儿存放现金、信用卡之类的东西吗？”

“很有可能在她的手提包里。”查利说。

警督转向他的一个手下。“警司，你查过了吗？”

“什么都没有，警督。手提包是空的。”

第74页

“那么惠特克先生，你知道你母亲的钱存在哪家银行吗？”我问。

“大通曼哈顿银行。”查利回答说。

“你现在给他们打电话可以吗？我们必须知道她的银行账户发生了什么。”

查利正要拿起电话的时候，电话响了。

“找你的，马利先生。”他说。

“嗨，纳特，是我。我打了电话，杰基现在可能就在酒店。”斯特拉说。

“乔来了吗？好的。告诉他在酒店外面等我。现在我有个主意，也许能行得通。帮我准备一个棕色的大纸包，在里面装满旧报纸和杂志，然后把它给乔。”

“没问题。”斯特拉答道。

时间紧迫。我搭乘开往市中心的列车到第 23 街。从地铁出来到地面上时，我看到乔在第八大道和第 22 街的拐角处等着，他的胳膊下面夹着那个包裹。他假装在读《每日新闻》。

切尔西·阿姆斯酒店曾经有过辉煌的日子。现在它看起来就跟其他廉价酒店一样。大厅的地面是脏兮兮的白色石头。前台的窗口后边一个人在用电脑办公，另外一个身材魁梧的家伙坐在前台对面的一张桌子旁。很显然，他在那里是为了防备出现任何麻烦。

第75页

“乔，你就待在门外边的街上，留点儿心。如果杰基想要逃跑，想尽办法拦住他。”

现在，我希望这个方法行得通。我迅速在包裹上写了一条留言，然后溜达到前台。

“有一位叫杰基·克莱顿的先生住在这里吗？”我问，“这是他的包裹。”

“你可以把它交给我。”前台接待员说。

“抱歉。特殊包裹，”我说，“必须由克莱顿先生签收。”

“我给房间打个电话。”

一分钟之后杰基下楼来到大厅，他紧张地左右张望。我向他挥舞着包裹。

“这是什么？”他说，“没有人会给我寄东西。”

“读一读，”我说，“这是给你的。”

杰基接过包裹。留言写着：“杰基——你的母亲奄奄一息，她想要见你。时间紧迫。”

他不知所措。我四处走动以堵住楼梯。杰基把包裹甩在我脸上，向前门跑去，结果却发现乔挡着他的路。随即他想要打乔。这个想法可不明智，特别是当你要打的这个家伙曾经是纽约市警察局重量级拳击手的时候。乔用他出了名的左直拳予以回击。杰基痛苦地大叫，向后倒在我怀里。

第76页

桌边那个身材魁梧的家伙站了起来。“住手，不然我就打911！”他喊道。

我把我的执照举到他面前。

“内森·马利，私家侦探。”我说，“这个人的母亲雇我来找他。”我转向杰基。“听着，杰基，你母亲病得很严重。我们是好人，不是怀斯曼的人。你母亲雇了我们来找你，你得相信我们。你看，让前台给贝尔维尤医院打电话——然后你就会相信我们了。”

杰基平静下来。他向前台的人点头示意，前台的人打电话给医院，随后把电话递给杰基。杰基慢慢地小声说道：“你们那里有叫安妮·克莱顿的病人吗？……你们有？……我这就过去。”杰基挂了电话，转过身来握住我们的手。“兄弟们，”他说，“我欠你们一句道歉。我还以为你们又是不速之客。我们走吧，我有20年没见过我妈妈了。”

第11章　玛莎·比安奇

第77页

医院差不多在城市另一端的正东方向。坐出租车是最明智的，我们在第八大道上找到了一辆。

“司机，去贝尔维尤医院。”我说。

在路上，我给杰基讲了他母亲的故事。

“所以妈妈这些年一直在街上流浪？”他问道。

“从她最后一次在牢房里见到你。”我说。

“我以前以为我什么都知道。”他说，“我觉得自己很坚强，不需要任何人。现在我更明白了，家人是你生命的一部分。过去我以为怀斯曼和弟兄们是家人，但是他们还不如这位司机像家人。只要你工作做得不错，就没问题。但是犯一次错误，你就会出局。”

“你犯了什么错，杰基？”我问道。

“我厌倦了成天提心吊胆提防警察，想过正常的生活。我想要一份普通的工作和一个可以属于我自己的地方。接着我开始想念我的家人。嘿，我们来得及吗？”

第78页

“我们能赶上。”我回答说。

“怀斯曼讨厌有人试图离开组织。”杰基继续说道，“过去的一年，我在谋生的同时还要躲着他。同时做这两件事情几乎不可能。我试图找到我母亲，还回到了布朗克斯，那是我长大的地方。一切都变了，我甚至认不出我住过的街道了。所有的旧国民住宅都被拆掉了，没人听说过安妮·克莱顿。”

我们停在医院外面。司机赚到了20美元的小费。前台的工作人员给费希尔医生打电话，她立即下来见杰基。

“杰基·克莱顿，失踪了很久的儿子，你会让你母亲非常开心的。”她说。

“她怎么样了，医生？”杰基问道。

“说实话，她活不了多久了，她很虚弱。这么多年流落街头，但是她在为你坚持着。进去的时候放松点儿，她很容易疲惫。我们现在就上去。”医生说。

杰基转向我说：“纳特，你能和我一起进去吗？”

“当然。”我说。

安妮在睡觉，她的嘴巴张着。医生轻轻地摇了一下她的手臂。“安妮，他回来了。”医生说。

第79页

她的脸上疲惫消失了，绽放出一个大大的笑容，泪水润湿了她的双眼。杰基握着她的手。

“啊！这不是我那个大傻儿子吗？这么多年了，终于回来看妈妈了。”她低声说。

“对不起，妈妈，我以前不是个好孩子。我已经改了。我一直在努力找你。”

“过来，让我抱紧你，这样好多了。”

第80页

“妈妈，纳特这个人了不起。他没有放弃。”

安妮转头冲着我笑。笑容背后，她已经筋疲力尽。

“纳特，我不知道该怎么感谢你。”她轻声说。

他们需要独处，但是我的一天还没有结束，我打电话给在东 43 街的斯特拉。

“纳特，进展如何？”她问。

“我们找到杰基了。”我说，“乔把他劝服了，他现在和安妮在一起。医生认为她活不了多久了。”

“可怜的女人。”斯特拉说。

“斯特拉，你这周已经做得足够多了。你找到了杰基。关好办公室的门，好好享受周末吧，我和乔要回惠特克公寓。”

我并不介意自己不过周末。闷热和疲惫开始向我袭来。医院外边有一排出租车，我和乔跳上了第一辆。

交通很堵，但是耽搁的时间正好可以用来思考。惠特克夫人睡前喝的东西里有什么？尸检能证明是喝的东西导致惠特克夫人死亡的吗？如果玛莎有力气毁掉家具，她应该能轻而易举谋杀惠特克夫人。但是怎么杀的呢？她看起来死得很平静，医生似乎也并不认为她的死亡有什么不同寻常的地方。出租车现在还在车流之中一动不动，这是一个补觉的机会。

第81页

到了世纪公寓，乔把我摇醒。公寓里，案发现场小组正准备撤离。查利·惠特克和威尔玛·帕特森正在检查文件。有一些文件又湿又脏。我不愿意去想玛莎在上边倒了什么。

“殡仪馆那边有什么消息吗？”我问警督。

“我们挺走运，先生。”他说，“他们还没有为惠特克夫人的葬礼做好准备，今天晚上将会进行尸检。这儿没有我们能做的事情了。”

查利·惠特克转向我。“你猜怎么着，”他说，“警督询问了所有的邻居。那天晚上玛莎破坏家具的时候，他们都听到了一些动静。他们以为是在开疯狂派对。我母亲什么时候开过疯狂派对？”

“可能是某种聚会。”我大笑道。

第82页

“锁没有任何问题，”查利继续说，“没人破门而入。看起来都是玛莎做的，马利先生。我母亲的大部分文件都在这里。啊！这张上有番茄酱。但是没有支票簿和信用卡。我给银行打过电话，幸运的是那儿有人能帮忙，我必须亲自过去。银行账号被透支了，看起来玛莎取走了好几万美元。”

“我想知道钱花在了哪儿。”我说。

“马利先生，找到那个女人，快一点儿。”查利说，“我要让她为自己的所作所为付出代价。”

“我们正在努力，惠特克先生。首先，我们需要彻底检查玛莎的房间。”

那条“去玩儿球了”的留言还在镜子上。

“可能是哪种‘球’呢，老大？”乔问。

“玛莎是棒球迷吗？”我问道，“答案一定在这里的某个地方。我们可以从检查这些书开始。”

一整个书架满满当当都是旧的侦探小说，它们看上去仿佛被读了一遍又一遍。这只能告诉我们她喜欢阅读。接着乔在床边地板上找到一本摊开的书。

“看看这本书，老大。”乔说，“玛莎一直在书上的某些段落做标记。”

第83页

这本书叫作《完美谋杀》，书页因年代久远而泛黄了。

我浏览了那本书，读了玛莎画横线的地方，一句话格外引起我的注意：

“我用枕头蒙住她的脸的时候，她踢了几下。但是这很快就彻底结束了。如果杀人如此容易，为什么不再做一次呢？他们说‘熟能生巧’。”

我拿给乔看。

“我觉得玛莎读得太多了。”他说。乔指着另一本书的内封：“看，她一直在练习怎么签惠特克夫人的名字。”

我把这本书给查利·惠特克看。

“你母亲是这样签名的吗？”我问道。

“是这样签的，玛莎就是用这种方式从我母亲的银行账号里成功取出了钱。”

我们回到玛莎的房间继续工作。没有行李箱，没有手提包，她自己的东西都不见了。随后我们开始研究乔在床底下找到的一摞度假宣传册。拉斯维加斯、奥奈达，还有大西洋城。

“在这些地方你只有一种球可以玩儿，”我对乔说，“而那就在赌场里。”

第84页

玛莎现在可能正在某个赌场里输掉惠特克夫人所有的钱。我们不知道她去了哪儿，也无法给一家赌场打电话问：“你们有没有在赌桌前见过这样一个人，她的长相符合以下描述……”即便有赌场真的同意帮忙，也可能会有很多中年妇女在输钱。这种人攒了一年的钱就为了度过一周的赌博假期。他们花光每一分钱，变成穷光蛋回家。

“你觉得她去哪儿了？”我问乔。

“我猜测是在近处而不是在远处。”他回答说。

“大西洋城最近。”我说，“你知道大西洋城有多少家赌场吗？至少十家，也许更多。”

房间里几乎没有任何东西能让你看出玛莎本人在这里生活过。我们搜寻了所有地方，想找到一张她的照片。没有可以给别人看的东西。我们唯一能做的是走访每一家赌场，直到我们找到她。

“所以现在怎么办，老大？”乔问道。

“开车去大西洋城要用几个小时。”我说，“我们可能需要在那里花上一整天时间。明天早上九点，把你的车开到办公室。确保你一定要休息好。”

第85页

我停顿了一会儿，有了一个想法。

“乔，这一切难道不会有点儿过于明显吗？如果玛莎真的想消失，为什么写下那条信息，还把书留下来？不知怎的，我觉得她想让我们找到她，她好像正在上演其中一部侦探小说。但是谁知道呢？”

天气似乎比以往更热了，我受够了。这种天气什么时候才能结束啊？明天又会是漫长的一天，而我的周末泡汤了。我睡前还要阅读点儿东西——《完美谋杀》。

第 12 章　大西洋城

第86页

那天晚上的大部分时间我都没睡而是在看书，并不是我想这样，只是在这么热的天我睡不着。日出时，我穿上了衣服放弃了。外面天气还算宜人，这不会持续很久。还有时间到贝尔维尤医院停留一下。我知道时间太早不适合看望安妮，但是也许护士能够告诉我安妮的最新情况。

医院里，医生把我带到了安妮的病房门前，并举起手指放到唇边。

“不要出声，”她低声说，“就看看吧。”

安妮·克莱顿和她的儿子杰基都在睡觉。杰基坐在床边，他的头枕在枕头上。安妮的手放在杰基的手里。

“他一直都没离开她。”护士说。

“安妮怎么样？”我问道。

她把我带到远离病房的地方，神色严肃。我在预想最糟糕的情况。

“我们无能为力了。”护士说，“现在只是等待的问题，可能是今天或是明天。”

第87页

“我很遗憾。”我说，“如果有任何新情况，请给我打电话。”

在东 43 街，我给警察局总部打电话，想看看惠特克夫人的尸检是否有什么结果。消息并没有让我感觉好一点儿。

“他们说她死于心脏病。如果是自然死亡，那就没什么可做的了。”

“药检结果如何？”我问。

“还太早，也许明天有结果。”

问题在于如何让纽约市警察局相信这是谋杀。如果药检显示在她体内的药物含量正常，我们就无法证明玛莎谋杀了她——除非她自己承认。

乔精神焕发地到了办公室。我呢，忍不住打哈欠。

“你为什么这么精神？”在他回车上的路上我问他。

“我晚上睡了个好觉，老大，正如你建议的那样。”乔回答说。

“好吧，我要困死了，到大西洋城叫醒我。”

我在后座躺下，很快便睡着了。那是好多天以来我睡得最香的觉。几个小时之后，我们沿着大西洋城高速公路进入城里，乔叫醒了我。

第88页

“你睡得像个婴儿，老大。”他说。

与城市不同，赌场是设计多样、色彩斑斓的漂亮建筑。我们停好车，沿着海边走，开始进赌场查看。每一家赌场的故事都一样，孤单落寞的人吻别大笔的钱。但是没有玛莎的踪影。我们到达金纱赌场的时候，已经查看过五家赌场了。

“不敢相信，老大！”乔说，“我从没见过这样的东西。”

进去的路上，我们经过一排巨大的白色石象。里面是一个梦幻般的世界。上面的灯仿佛璀璨的星云，舒缓的音乐在演奏着，深黑色木头、深色地毯，到处闪烁着金银般的光芒。刚过中午，人们就挤到了轮盘赌桌前。

“在那儿，乔！是玛莎。”

她就在那儿，坐在两位老妇人中间。在玛莎旁边她们显得很娇小。玛莎面前有成堆的色彩艳丽的赌场筹码。她玩儿得很大，已经把筹码放到了数字 7、14、21 和 28 上。球射出去后转来转去，最终停在了数字 7 上。玛莎一边尖叫，一边大笑。

第89页

“又是我赢！”她喊道，“就是这么玩儿，我知道我不会输！”

我再也看不下去了，走向她。

“玛莎，”我说，“我们得聊聊。”

“哟，这不是私家侦探先生本人吗？”她回答说，“我还想你们什么时候能到这里。走开，我正赢钱呢。”

她开始把更多的筹码放在桌上。够了，我把它们推到地上。

“嘿，你以为你在干什么？”她喊道。

“劳驾，”我身后有一个声音说，“有什么问题吗？”一只手重重地落在我的肩膀上。我转过身，是一个穿着黑色制服、身材高大魁梧的家伙，他的上衣上别着赌场工作证。

“不要打扰这位女士，出去，否则我就报警了。”他说。

我举起我的私家侦探执照。现在我必须快速行动，一切都指望着玛莎承认谋杀。

“纳特·马利，私家侦探。”我说，“这位女士花的是偷来的钱。钱是她从雇主那里偷的，而她杀害了雇主。对吧，玛莎？钱和药的事我们全都知道了。就像你特别喜欢的那部侦探小说里说的那样。”

第90页

轮盘赌桌前一片寂静，人们张大嘴盯着我们。我举起玛莎的书。

“你真是个聪明人！”玛莎说，“我还想你要花多长时间，比我预期的要快。我确实是从书中得到灵感的。我在她的热巧克力里多放了几片安眠药，然后就不再会有‘玛莎做这个，玛莎做那个’了。只需要把枕头蒙在她的头上。她踢了几下，但是几秒钟之内就全都结束了，小菜一碟。而且她的面容看上去完好无损。所有事情都像书里说的那样发生了。只是更快，更容易。这是她自己的错，她的遗嘱里没有我！”

“你读得太多了。”我说。

那个穿制服的人开始明白发生了什么。

“你们最好来一下办公室。”他说，“你需要我报警吗，马利先生？”

“非常乐意。”我说，“你能帮忙把所有的筹码都收集起来吗？那是偷来的钱。”

又过了几个小时，我们才在大西洋城警察局总部办完事。玛莎又向新泽西州警察局供认了所有的事。她没有一点儿悔意，事实上，她看起来很享受这一切。

第91页

“现在怎么办，警督？”玛莎问道，“你们会把我关到牢房里吗？”

“是的，直到纽约市警察局来接你。”警督回复说，“警司，把她带走。现在，马利先生，我要跟奥尔登伯格警监通话。这是纽约市警察局的事。”

已经到了傍晚，我们必须回纽约。我可以在路上打几个电话。我一整天都在惦记安妮。我给贝尔维尤医院的费希尔医生打通了电话。她认为安妮撑不过今晚，而杰基一直在找我。没时间可浪费。

另一个电话打给查利·惠特克，他正在等我们的消息。幸运的是，他还在世纪公寓。

“惠特克先生？”我说，“我们在大西洋城找到玛莎了。”

“你们找到她了？她杀了我母亲？”查利问道。

“她全都承认了，”我告诉他，“就像我想的那样。她像个百万富翁一样在赌场赌博。”

第92页

“钱不重要，”查利说，“我想让她为自己所做的事情付出代价。”

“别担心，她会的。”

我们到达医院时，天已经黑了。杰基正在安妮的病房外等我们。

“你们太棒了，为我们做了这么多。”杰基说。

“别客气，安妮怎么样了？”我问。

“妈妈快不行了，她现在昏迷不醒。她聊了过去的事。至少现在她没有痛苦。”

“我们会陪着你，杰基。这种时候你需要朋友在身边。我认识你母亲很久了，我想在她离开的时候在场。”

杰基回到病房里。我们一直等到凌晨，看着时钟的指针一圈一圈地转动。在夜晚的那个时刻，医院是个非常奇怪的地方。奄奄一息的人在一小时又一小时地等待，等待那个死亡的时刻。凌晨2点

30分，护士叫费希尔医生。快速检查之后，她挥手让我们进去。安妮的呼吸现在变得缓慢而不规律。最终，呼吸停止了。杰基始终握着他母亲的手。

“我很难过，杰基。她走了。”医生说。

第93页

杰基抬头看着我们。“她从来没有对我放弃希望。”他说，“你们能给我一点儿时间让我单独和妈妈待一会儿吗？”

病房外，乔认真地看着我。

“纳特！你流眼泪了。”他说。

“眼泪？我？不，一定是什么东西进到眼睛里了。”

其实他是对的。安妮的死深深地震动了我，比我预想的更深。但是惠特克夫人死的时候，我却没有任何感觉。十分钟后，杰基出来了。

“我们送你回家吧，杰基。”我悲伤地说，“我会怀念在大中央车站和安妮的早晨闲聊。”

第 13 章　雨

第94页

又是一个周一的早晨。我走出大中央车站到第42街时，天空乌云密布。你几乎能够感受到空气中的电流，终于要变天了。我到办公室时，豆大的雨点开始砸在人行道的路面上。

斯特拉像往常一样坐在她的桌旁。

“纳特，有一名客人。”她说。

“谁？”我问。

“去看看。”

“为什么这么神秘?”

天空突然被点亮，随即一片黑暗，雷声大作。办公室里有一张我再熟悉不过的脸。又一声雷鸣，大雨滂沱，暴风雨开始了。

“奥尔登伯格！你真是知道怎么吓唬人。”

“我喜欢这样，马利。”奥尔登伯格说，“你知道天气不好的时候犯罪通常会减少吗?”

“你来这儿不是为了谈论天气的。你到底为什么会在这里?”

第95页

奥尔登伯格想和杰基·克莱顿聊聊。他需要杰基的帮助好把怀斯曼送进监狱。作为回报，警察局承诺清掉杰基的案底，让他过上新生活。杰基相信我，所以他们让我去安排会面。

奥尔登伯格离开后，暴风雨更猛烈了。雨水汇成小河在街道上流淌。来了更多访客，斯特拉带进来两名工人。

“纳特，这次是让人惊喜的好事。”斯特拉说。

“马利先生，我们是来装空调的。”其中一名工人说。

“难以置信。为什么你们上周不来呢?”我问。

他们开始安装空调机组时发出的碰撞声和敲打声让人几乎无法工作。也许我该搬到气候更宜人的地方，比如阿拉斯加。在安克雷奇，有谁会需要空调呢?现在并不是接待另一位访客的最佳时机，威尔玛·帕特森到了。她想让我安排明早在她办公室与杰基会面，宣读他母亲的遗嘱。随即，电话响了。工人们那边传来更多碰撞声和敲打声。

“你们这些家伙能停一会儿吗?”我问，“我是马利，抱歉。”

第96页

“我是查利·惠特克，我需要你的建议。我刚跟奥尔登伯格警监谈过，警方不确定玛莎是否会因谋杀罪而受到审判。”

“继续。”我说。

“钱的方面没有问题，”查利说，“支票簿和信用卡都在她的手提包里。她确实偷了所有的钱。但是至于谋杀，这个女人疯了，她似乎生活在侦探小说的虚幻世界里。没人能确定她说的是真话还是在讲故事。尸检结果也没有帮上我们什么忙。药检结果没有确切发现，所以仍旧是自然死亡。你有什么建议吗，纳特？”

“因为偷盗和对公寓的所作所为，她会在监狱里待很长时间。”我说道，“当她取光了你母亲的银行账户时，很清楚自己在做什么。这是个棘手的案子，惠特克先生。看起来她会被判盗窃罪，而不是谋杀罪。但是无论哪种罪，她都会蹲很久的监狱。而且纽约州的监狱生活可没那么轻松。我会接受奥尔登伯格所说的。你我都清楚她犯有谋杀罪，但是让别人相信这些是另一回事。”

“好吧，这不是我想听到的。”查利说，“但是我觉得现在我们也没什么能做的了。不管怎么说，如果她没有被判谋杀罪，他们可以早点儿把妈妈的遗体送回来举行葬礼。”

第97页

又一个电话。这次是杰基，他告诉我安妮的葬礼将于周六上午十一点在昆斯区举行。我答应出席。杰基说他在明天上午十点能赶到威尔玛的办公室听他母亲的遗嘱。我不确定他是否会接受奥尔登伯格的建议。

“还有一件事，杰基。”我说，“我知道现在说不合适，但是奥尔登伯格警监想见你。”

“我不喜欢听到这样的声音，纳特。”杰基说道。

“稍等，杰基。他们想抓怀斯曼，但是他们需要日期、时间、名字、地点等信息。作为回报，他们将不再追究你过去为怀斯曼做的所有事情。这会是你需要的全新的开始。”

“这要好好想想，纳特，”杰基说，“我明天给你答复。”

办公室里这么吵，根本无法工作。“我要有一段很长的午餐休息时间。”我跟工人们喊道，“这儿有钥匙。如果你们在我们回来之前结束，就把钥匙留在大厅。如果那些机组不能运转……”

第98页

“相信我们，先生，”其中一名工人说，“我们睡着觉都能做这个。”

漫长的午休持续了快一个下午。上周发生了一系列事情后，我觉得越来越累。我留下斯特拉锁门，逃回昆斯区去睡觉了。

第二天早上，曼哈顿市中心在暴风雨过后显得清新整洁，湛蓝的天空万里无云。这又会是一个大热天吗？接着我记起来了，我已经花了七百美元装了空调。那些机组最好能起作用。当我走进东43街的办公室时，感觉空气像是结了冰。

“这是怎么回事？”我问道，“西伯利亚吗？”

“对不起，纳特，”斯特拉说，“只不过是空调出了点儿小问题。”

“好吧，我宁愿热死也不愿意冻死。”

“少来，纳特！我已经尽力了。我不能永远不出错。我只是个普通人，又不是女超人。哦，对了，威尔玛·帕特森打过电话。你能九点半到她的办公室吗？”

在威尔玛的办公室，有一摞文件需要我签字。惠特克夫人留给我的所有遗产现在都将转给查利·惠特克和他的妹妹贝蒂·奥斯本，两人平分。最开始就该是这样。

第99页

“纳特，有个关于你费用的问题。”威尔玛说。

“我会让斯特拉把我的账单发给惠特克先生。”我说。

“不必了，”她说，“他告诉我把这个给你。他希望这么多够了。”她递给我一个装满钱的信封。

何止是够了，非常仁义。现在我感觉空调的事没有那么糟了。到了十点，我、杰基、威尔玛和斯特拉围坐在安妮的金属盒子边。威尔玛拿出钥匙把它打开。

“克莱顿先生，”她说，“你妈妈的遗嘱很简单。盒子里的所有东西都是你的，你可以自由支配。”

盒子里是一摞文件。最上面放着一个信封，写着“给我的儿子，杰基”。杰基打开它，然后大声读出信的内容。

给我亲爱的儿子，杰基：

我不知道你在哪儿，但是这么多年我一直为你保存着这个。一份来自你从不认识的父亲的礼物。他是个成功的商人。如果这里的东西值点儿钱的话，用它给你自己一个未来。

爱你的妈妈

“她一直惦记着我。”杰基说，“但是这些文件都是什么？这张纸条又是什么意思？”

第100页

威尔玛从杰基手中拿过文件和纸条，仔细地翻阅了一遍。

“克莱顿先生，这张纸条一定是你父亲写的。听着：

安妮，对孩子而言，我从来算不上是个真正的父亲。这里有些钱能帮忙解决吃穿问题，还有将来用得上的东西。留着这些股票凭证，有一天，它们可能会值很多钱。

你的汤姆”

“这个汤姆是谁？”杰基问道。

“答案一定在这里面。”威尔玛说。她仔细地检查了文件，直到找到那些股票凭证。“你母亲对你真的很好。看到这些凭证了吗？这股票可能值几万美元。一切都安排好了。股票在你母亲名下，是被转赠给她的，由……难以置信：汤姆·惠特克！”

“这是怎么回事？”杰基问道。

“杰基，我想我知道你父亲是谁了。我记得安妮告诉过我她做过办公室清洁工，她在那里遇到了公司的老板。那个男人就是汤姆·惠特克，一个成功的商人，惠特克航空的董事长。”

第101页

我的钱包里还有一份《每日新闻》报道的复印件，上面有汤姆·惠特克的照片。

“就是他，杰基，留着它。这还不是全部，杰基。你有家人，一个同父异母的哥哥和一个同父异母的姐姐，查利·惠特克和贝蒂·奥斯本。他们住在纽约州北部。”

杰基沉默了一会儿，然后他转向威尔玛。

“帕特森夫人，有一些事情我必须知道，这很重要。如果妈妈没有见到我就去世了，会发生什么？或者我拒绝见她，或者如果纳特没有找到我，又或者如果我死了。如果、如果、如果……”

“为了防止那样的事情发生，安妮在遗嘱中额外加了一部分。”威尔玛解释说，“出售股票的钱将用来帮助无家可归的女人。我觉得安妮并不真正知道它的价值。”

“帕特森夫人，你能帮我保管这些股票凭证吗?”杰基问道，“我需要时间思考。”

盒子里还有其他的东西，几张黑白家庭照片，一位年轻的母亲和她怀中笑着的开心的婴儿，小学的班级合影，儿时的生日聚会，在科尼艾兰的家庭旅行。接下来是彩色照片，一个充满活力的少年拿着一根棒球棒。翻看这些照片的时候，杰基的眼睛里闪烁着泪光。这个可怜的家伙在过去几天经历了太多，失去了母亲，找到了一个新家。一个前途黯淡的家伙现在有了希望。杰基重新忆起他的童年，我们静静地坐着。几分钟之后，他准备说话了。现在他看起来平静而自信。

第102页

“纳特、帕特森夫人，”杰基开始说，“我决定了。帕特森夫人，你能帮我查一下这股票值多少钱吗? 妈妈医院的账单需要支付，还有纳特先生付出了这么多，也应该拿到报酬。”

“当然可以。”威尔玛说。

“还有纳特，你说我有同父异母的哥哥和姐姐。我真的很想见见他们，他们是家人。你认识惠特克家的人，所以你可以安排一次见面吗? 还有一件事，我一直在想你昨天说的事情。答案是‘可以’。如果我想和过去划清界限，我必须这么做。给奥尔登伯格警监打电话吧。如果能让我摆脱怀斯曼，把他关进牢房里，我愿意按他希望的去做。”

“交给我吧，杰基。我们葬礼上见。”

第 14 章　安妮·克莱顿中心

第103页

出席安妮葬礼的不足十人，其中包括安妮的好朋友埃莉和利昂娜，还有查利·惠特克和贝蒂·奥斯本。我把杰基介绍给了查利和贝蒂，直到我离开的时候他们还在一起聊天。

惠特克夫人盛大的葬礼一两天之后在奥尔巴尼举行，出席的有家人和几位汤姆·惠特克旧日的酒友。我去参加葬礼是因为我觉得我应该去，并非出于自愿。令我再次感到惊奇的是又看到杰基·克莱顿和查利以及贝蒂在一起，也许他找到了他的家人。

七月中旬以后日子变得更加清净，我甚至去度了假。在那之后，我只是继续接手日常工作——离婚案件或是寻找失踪的人。没有什么可让人兴奋的，但我不是在抱怨，我更喜欢这样。快到九月底的时候，我收到了纽约州监狱寄来的一封信。是玛莎写的，但看起来像是一个孩子的笔迹。

第104页

致私家侦探纳特·马利先生：

在过去两个月，我收获的快乐比过去二十年都多。我很喜欢待在监狱这里，每个人都很照顾我，生活有了改变，人们很善良。我和狱友相处十分融洽，她是因为谋杀罪被关进来的。

玛莎

所以玛莎很享受监狱里的生活。铁窗后的生活一定适合她的性格。以她的体格和力气，她多半不会受其他狱友的欺负。从她的信里看得出她们对她挺好——比惠特克夫人对她要好。不管怎么说，社会可以免受玛莎·比安奇的伤害了。

炎热的夏天终于过去了，而我正享受着我最喜欢的季节——秋天。中央公园的树已经变成了红色和金色的海洋。办公室的生活一如既往。秋去冬来。办公室里，斯特拉对寒冷的抱怨和去年夏天对炎热的抱怨一样多。春天来临的时候，我们都很高兴。

那是春天的一个早上，我惊喜地发现我的邮件中有一封邀请信，是第 125 街上安妮·克莱顿中心的开业邀请。我和斯特拉几乎难以相信。这么说杰基还是找到了回报他母亲的方式。

第105页

开业那天早上，我、斯特拉和乔一起坐车向北到哈莱姆区。中心外面是一群看上去身份显赫的人。有社区领导和当地政客，还有报纸和当地电视台的记者们。杰基·克莱顿、查利·惠特克和贝蒂·奥斯本站在正门那里。

查利·惠特克先发言。

“女士们、先生们，欢迎大家来参加安妮·克莱顿中心的开业典礼。这栋楼为城市里无家可归的女性提供舒适的房间。无论何种肤色或是宗教信仰，每个人都会受到欢迎。入住这个中心的女性有一个共同的特点——没有住处。我和我的妹妹，以及我同父异母的弟弟杰基·克莱顿最近都失去了母亲，这栋大楼是为了纪念她们的。”

随后杰基向前迈步。从我上次见他以后，他有了改变。这不是七月份我遇到的那个担惊受怕的出租车司机了。他讲话的时候，神态和声音都很自信。

第107页

“谢谢你，查利。我的母亲安妮·克莱顿在这座城市的街头生活了二十多年。她需要爱和关心，而作为一个年轻人，我没能给她那份爱和关心。如果曾经有这样的一个中心，也许她就不用在城市的街头流浪了。我真诚地希望这个中心能够在接下来的很多年为像我母亲一样的女性提供帮助。”

接着，查利和贝蒂与杰基站到一起。贝蒂开始讲话。

“最后，我们要对一个人表示特别的感谢，他的努力付出使这一切成为可能。没有他，我们可能永远不会相遇。他就是安妮·克莱顿的一位老朋友，纳特·马利先生。”

她指向我，电视摄像机同时转向我。记者的采访随之而来。我与杰基和惠特克兄妹拍了一张合影，登在了报纸上。这会是一个精彩的、充满人情味儿的故事。最终，我们得以脱身。杰基带我们进了一间办公室。

“我们都对你和你的搭档们所做的一切表示衷心的感谢。”杰基说，“葬礼之后，我和查利、贝蒂一起聊天，发现我们有很多共同之处。”

“奇怪，布朗克斯遇见上西区。”我说。

第108页

“你看，我们都失去了母亲，而且我们都以不同的方式度过了艰难的童年。我总是在街上遇到麻烦。”杰基说。

“而我们有一个冷漠的、不懂关爱的父亲。”查利说，“我还记得在那间公寓里长大的感觉，和他过去对妈妈做的事情。”

“遇到我妈妈的老朋友埃莉和利昂娜的时候，我开始思考，”杰基说，“如何用妈妈的钱帮助像她们一样的人。我跟查利和贝蒂谈了这个想法。”

“公寓是我们的，但是经历了发生的这一切之后，我们再也不想踏进那里。”查利说，“我觉得我们必须要做些什么。杰基的想法是把我们的钱凑到一起，做点儿事情帮助人们改善生活。很辛苦，但是一切都是值得的。”

“我还能说什么呢？这地方是个了不起的成果。”我说，“安妮从没放弃过对你的希望，她是对的，杰基。”

最终我们说了再见。走在第 125 街的阳光下，我开始思考。我之前曾说过，我见到过这座城市最优越和最不堪的生活。我错了，这个中心是我见过的最好的。尽管我的心情很复杂。安妮曾经住在纽约的街头，而她有足够的钱可以找个安身之所。她本可以不必受这些苦。

第109页

斯特拉摸摸我的手。

“你还好吗，纳特？”她问道。

“只是在思考。安妮·克莱顿中心，一样能纪念她的东西，她死后就像还活着一样。要是她知道股票的价值就好了，死前她本可以享受生活的。”

“她没能享受到生活应有的公平待遇。但是其他人会的，纳特，其他人会的。”